HEADWAY

WORKBOOK **ADVANCED**

John & Liz Soars

Oxford University Press

Note to Students and Teachers

The exercises in Units 1–12 of this Workbook are presented in the following order:

– further practice of the input presented in the Language Study section of *Headway Advanced* Student's Book
– writing input and/or practice
– pronunciation work
– vocabulary
– multi-word verbs

This order is for ease of reference only. The exercises can, of course, be studied in the order that suits you best.

As well as providing a wide range of language practice, the Workbook also contains input additional to that in the Student's Book. This can be studied either at home or in the classroom.

Each unit contains a section which focuses on developing the writing skill, while there is an exercise on multi-word verbs in Unit 1 and in every even-numbered unit. The Vocabulary section of every odd-numbered unit includes exercises on idioms and dependent prepositions.

At the back of the Workbook there are three appendices which contain reference lists of multi-word verbs, dependent prepositions, and linking words.

John and Liz Soars

CONTENTS

UNIT 1

1 Information before and after a noun

Rewrite the following short sentences in the form of one longer sentence. Remember to include all the information. The table on page 134 of the Student's Book will help you.

a. Ford has produced a new car. It's a saloon car. It has four doors. Its top speed is over 120 mph.

_____

_____

b. I'm going on a holiday. It will last for three weeks. It'll be quite an adventure. We're going to drive through the Sahara Desert.

_____

_____

c. Aitken's biography of Churchill has met with great critical acclaim. It's in three volumes. It was written in the last years of the statesman's life.

_____

_____

d. Richard Stallman has signed a contract. The contract will last for two years. Richard Stallman makes records. The contract is with EMI. He's going to produce two albums a year.

_____

_____

_____

e. He wrote his employer a letter. It was fifteen pages long. In it, he explained why he had resigned.

_____

_____

f. She's going to do a course. It will take three years. At the end she will get a degree. It's at Sussex University.

_____

_____

g. The first prize in the competition is a cruise. The cruise will take forty-eight days. It will go round the world. The winner will stay in a first class cabin. The liner is the Queen Elizabeth II.

_____

_____

h. We have just bought a table. It's six feet long. It's made of pine. It's for having picnics on.

_____

_____

i. The judge gave her a sentence. He sent her to prison for three years. She had kidnapped a millionaire's son.

_____

_____

j. The Midland Trading Company have made a bid. They want to take over the textile manufacturer, AMA. They have offered £48 million. They made the offer at the last minute.

_____

_____

2 Compound nouns

Match words in column **A** with words in column **B** to form compound nouns. Sometimes there is more than one possibility. Use a dictionary to check whether they are written as one word, two words, or hyphenated. Write out the compound nouns in column **C**.

A	B	C
	colour	
	conditioning	
	drill	
	mark	
	melon	
air	ship	
	scape	
water	raid	
	work	
fire	shed	
	slide	
land	escape	
	lift	
	arms	
	fall	
	wings	
	brigade	
	space	

_____. Isn't she making some clothes at the moment?

c. **A** I never see Lionel these days. How is he?

  B We often _____. He's fine. He's into business management at the moment.

d. I asked him to help me start the car, but he

  _____. Isn't that mean of him?

e. **A** When are you going to get the car serviced?

  B It _____ ,_____! Can't you feel how smoothly it's going?

f. **A** Oh no! The spare tyre's flat! Why didn't you check it before we set out?

  B I thought I _____. Sorry.

g. **A** No, I haven't got a copy of the book you want.

  B Really? I thought you _____. I was sure I saw a copy on your shelves the other day.

h. **A** He never seems to be listening when you talk to him.

  B I'm sure he _____. He just doesn't respond immediately, that's all.

i. **A** Clare spent all that money she won on new clothes for the family.

  B I _____ _____. I'd have saved some.

j. I hope Jack likes playing cards. Then we could

  have a game this evening. If he _____ , we

  _____.

k. My children always let me know what time they

  expect to be back. If they _____, I'd always be worrying about where they were.

l. **A** My bank statement says I'm overdrawn. The bank must have made a mistake.

  B They _____ _____. It's all done by computer. Are you sure you worked it out properly?

Avoiding repetition

3 Avoiding repetition of the verb

Fill each gap in the following sentences with an auxiliary verb or a modal verb. Sometimes you will need to add **not**. (Contractions such as **can't** count as one word.)

a. Are you thinking of driving to work today? I

  _____ if I were you. It's very foggy. Why not take the train?

b. **A** Did you take my scissors?

  B I _____, but Anne _____

Writing

4 Links between parts of sentences

In the following text, one or two (but not more) of the linking words and phrases are correct, and the others are incorrect. Underline the correct ones.

Write a similar letter of application for the scholarship, giving information about yourself and your background, and why you would like the scholarship.

rua Quintino Bocaiuva
47 apt 602
Floresta CEP 90000
Porto Alegra
Brazil
12 December 1988

Mr James Kennedy
Director
The Benson Institute
15, Kimberley Way
London W1P 4ST

Dear Mr Kennedy

The Principal at the college where I work suggested that I should write to you (a) | for to / in order to / so as to / so that | find out more information

about the Benson Scholarship for advanced students of English, (b) | as / because / for / due to | he feels I could be a suitable candidate for

this particular scholarship.

I first visited England eight years ago (c) | then / when / as / while | I was twenty-one years old, (d) | immediately after graduating / as soon as graduated / following I graduated / having graduated | in

Chemistry at the University of Rio. (e) | At first / Then / At the beginning / In the beginning | I could speak no English. (f) | Despite this, / Nevertheless, / But / Although | I managed

to find some work.

(g) | So / Thus / Unfortunately, / Meanwhile, | I could only afford language classes twice a week, and (h) | owing to / consequently / as a result, / so that | I had to rely on my own

resources to acquire as much English as possible. (i) | Really, / In fact, / Presently, / Actually, | to my surprise I managed to pass Cambridge First

Certificate after only two years, and (j) | following, / subsequently, / after, / lately, | I took the Proficiency exam (k) | since / just before / prior to / on | leaving England four

years ago. (l) | On / No sooner / Having / When | returning home, I was lucky enough to find a job teaching English at the Academy School. I have

thoroughly enjoyed my involvement in the profession. (m) | But / In addition, / However, / Moreover, | I now feel the time has come for me to re-acquaint

myself with an English-speaking environment (n) | to / in order to / so that / so | maintain the standard of my English. (o) | That is why / Furthermore, / On the other hand, / Moreover, |

I would very much like to pursue my growing interest in English literature.
I look forward to hearing from you.
Yours sincerely,

Ms Manola Suarez

5 A poem – 'Another day'

Read the following poem, checking the meaning and pronunciation of any unknown words.

Another Day

Boys shout,
Girls giggle,
Pencils write,
Squiggle squiggle.
Get it wrong,
Cross it out,
Bell's gone,
All out!

Balls bounce,
Hands clap,
Skipping ropes,
Slap slap.
Hand-stands,
By the wall,

Sara Williams,
Best of all.
Boys fight,
Girls flee,
Teacher's gone
And spilt
His tea.
Clatter bang!
Big din,
Whistle goes,
All in!

All quiet,
No sound,
Hear worms,
Underground.
Chalk squeaks,

Clock creeps,
Head on desk,
Boy sleeps.

Home time,
Glory be,
Mum's got,
Chips for tea.
Warm fire,
Full belly,
Sit down,
Watch telly.

Bed time,
Creep away,
Dream until,
Another day.

John Cunliffe

After reading

Answer the following questions.

a. What is the poem about?
b. How old do you think the poet is?
c. Where does each verse take place?
d. Underline the words in the poem which you consider to be onomatopoeic.
e. How would you describe the rhythm of the poem?

Now read it aloud as fast as you can, with expression to suit the mood of each verse.

Groups of consonants

When three or more consonant sounds come together, it can be hard to pronounce them all.

Practise reading out loud the phonemic transcripts of the following extracts from the poem, and write the actual words next to them.

a. /gɜːlzgɪgl/ _____
b. /penslzraɪt/ _____
c. /belzgɒn/ _____
d. /bɔːlzbaʊns/ _____
e. /hænzklæp/ _____
f. /hænstænz/ _____
g. /gɜːlzfliː/ _____
h. /tʃɔːkskwiːks/ _____
i. /mʌmzgɒ(t)tʃɪpsfətiː/ _____

Word linking

Draw a line to show where the word links are in the following extracts from the poem.

Get it wrong.

a. Cross it out.
b. All out!
c. Best of all.
d. Teacher's gone And spilt His tea. /tiːtʃəzgɒnənspɪltɪztiː/
e. Head on desk.
f. Creep away.
g. Dream until Another day.

6 Idioms – their origins

It is difficult to use idioms accurately and appropriately in a foreign language. Before you can use them you need to be able to recognize and understand them.

Inferring meaning

In the following story there are ten idioms in italics. Look at the context and try to work out the meaning.

My mother was a writer of historical novels, and everyone said I was *a chip off the old block* when I started writing short stories as a teenager. My mother was in fact my sternest critic, and *gave short shrift* to my first attempts at writing. My stories obviously didn't *come up to scratch*. She had *learned the ropes* slowly and painfully over the years, and was determined that it should not be too easy for me.

However, she did help me to *lick* my first book of short stories *into shape*, but when it came to getting it published, she refused to *pull strings* with any of her publishing friends, and I had to approach all the publishing houses myself. We sent it to nine of them, and were *on tenterhooks* waiting for the replies. There were eight letters of refusal, but we were *over the moon* when Duxford's Press said they were considering publication. Unfortunately, we got some very bad news. They accused me of plagiarism, saying that my plots and characters were identical to some American writer's. Well, I'd never heard of him! That really *upset the apple cart*. They said they couldn't publish, so it was *back to the drawing board*. I slaved away at a new collection of stories, and it was another two years before I finally saw my name in print.

Matching

Match the above idioms to their respective dictionary definitions.

a. very pleased

b. in a state of anxious suspense

c. give brief and unwilling attention to something

d. spoil someone's plans

e. learn how to deal with a particular task, job or problem

f. exert influence to obtain a favour

g. be like one of one's parents in character or behaviour

h. be of a satisfactory standard

i. start a project again because the first attempt was unsuccessful

j. improve something so that it is ready for use, or presentable

Origins of idioms

Knowing where idioms come from often helps you to remember their meanings. Read these ten extracts from the book *Everyday Phrases, their Origins and Meanings* by Neil Ewart.

A chip off the old block is used to describe a son resembling his father, or inheriting his talents. It was made famous when Edmund Burke (1729-1797), the great statesman, orator and writer, exclaimed excitedly, after listening to the first speech in the British Parliament of William Pitt the Younger, in 1781, that 'he was not merely a chip off the old block, but the old block itself'.

To give short shrift to anyone today means to deal with them swiftly and curtly, and generally to treat them in an unsympathetic manner.

In the Middle Ages when justice was harsh, and executions frequent, a condemned man would barely be given a chance to say anything before sentence of hanging was passed.

Later, in the 16th century, when 'short shrift' was introduced it came to mean the short time, of a few minutes, allowed before the execution of a criminal, during which he was allowed to make his confession to a priest and be granted absolution for his sins.

To come up to scratch is to do what is expected of one, and not shirk one's duties.

In the days of bare-fisted boxing matches, before there was a proper ring, contestants had to toe a line scratched on the ground between them, or 'come up to scratch', before the fight could start.

Competitors in races also had to 'come up to scratch' - the line marked out, or scratched, from which the race would commence.

To know the ropes was an expression coined in the days of sailing ships when a knowledge of all the intricacies of the ship's rigging was vital. Sailors needed to know every rope, and how it should be handled and used. The phrase subsequently came into use during the 19th century to refer to anyone who knew exactly how to handle something. Such a person was regarded as an expert in their craft or profession.

To lick into shape — When hunters in times past saw mother bears licking what appeared to be the shapeless mass of their newly-born cubs they assumed that she was, literally, shaping them with her tongue. Bear cubs weigh almost nothing, and are ridiculously small compared with their parents so it would have been difficult to see what the mother bear was really doing, unless studied at extremely close quarters. Although subsequent generations know that she was not shaping, but cleaning them, the phrase which is of 15th-century origin, is still widely used when anyone is making anything, or anybody, more presentable.

To pull strings — To have on a string. The word 'string' is derived from the Anglo-Saxon *strang*, meaning strong. *To pull strings* is to use one's influence behind the scenes to gain an advantage, by manipulating someone, or something. *To have someone on a string* implies that one has control. Both phrases are associated with puppets whose movements are manipulated and controlled through the use of strings.

To be on tenterhooks is to be in a state of suspense, anxiety, or full of expectation. Fully stretched and under strain, in fact, as the word comes from the Latin 'tendre' meaning 'to stretch'.

The expression comes from cloth-making and weaving in which the finished material is stretched on a frame known as a 'tenter' with the cloth being attached to it at the edges by means of 'tenter hooks'.

Over the moon is to be delighted with something, or with the situation one finds oneself in. When people are extremely happy, or sportsmen achieve a victory, they frequently jump for joy, just as the cow did in the famous 18th-century nursery rhyme when it jumped over the moon. If a cow can do it, the implication is that humans can also.

To upset the apple cart — This phrase is first recorded in use in 1796. It was adapted for everyday use to describe the spoiling of someone's carefully laid plans, or some unexpected intervention which leads to a state of disorder and confusion.

Until the 19th century roads were generally rough and streets were narrow. For country people, the mere act of getting themselves and their goods to market safely over considerable distances was quite an achievement. One can imagine how annoyed they must have been when the carts containing their precious produce were toppled over, particularly if they had perishable items such as apples, which would become damaged when scattered and ruin the hopes of a profitable sale.

Back to the drawing board — Although the best inventions are often the simplest, none are easy, and long hours, frequently adding up to many years, of relentless work and calculations are necessary before success or perfection is achieved. When things go wrong, it is often necessary to make a fresh start from the beginning and, as most plans and inventions have to be drawn and worked out on paper first, the phrase for starting anything afresh, 'Back to the drawing board', came into general use.

7 Dependent prepositions

Put the correct preposition into each gap.

Education

When my grandmother was at school, she had to learn everything (a) _____ heart, and even years later she could recite countless poems (b) _____ memory. She was discouraged (c) _____ thinking (d) _____ herself, and concentrated simply (e) _____ learning facts. The teachers were very strict (f) _____ pupils in those days. My grandfather confided (g) _____ me that he was expelled (h) _____ school (i) _____ playing truant just once.
It is always worthwhile for governments to invest (j) _____ education. Nobody should be deprived (k) _____ a good education, and everybody should benefit (l) _____ it. Nothing can compensate (m) _____ a bad start in life. Pupils (n) _____ public schools still account (o) _____ many of the students at Oxford and Cambridge University. Until quite recently these universities seemed to be prejudiced (p) _____ pupils from state schools. Many people objected very strongly (q) _____ this and at last things are changing.

I had no intention (r) _____ staying (s) _____ at university after I had finished my first degree. I finally succumbed (t) _____ parental pressure, but only (u) _____ protest, and carried out research (v) _____ the life of Baudelaire.

Multi-word verbs

8 Literal and idiomatic meanings

Multi-word verbs are also known as phrasal verbs, and consist of a verb + preposition/adverb.

Sometimes their meaning is literal, sometimes it is idiomatic, and sometimes the same multi-word verb can have several meanings, both literal and idiomatic.

They can therefore be used as puns (plays on words). Can you understand the following puns?

(*An advertisement for an airline*)
Splash out on the beach, not on the fare!

(*A children's joke*)
A Why are airline passengers so nice to each other?
B I don't know. Why are they?
A Because they don't want to fall out!

(*The comedian Groucho Marx to a lady*)
'If I said you had a beautiful body, would you hold it against me?'

You will read an article from the *Independent* newspaper by the humourist, Miles Kington. The article is in the form of an English language lesson on multi-word verbs, with the teacher trying to explain, and the student asking questions.

Before reading

1 Read the following sentences and try to work out the meaning of the multi-word verb. Some you will know, others are more difficult.

a. My sister has written, asking if we can **put** her **up** for a few days whilst she's in London.
b. Paul was left ten thousand pounds in his grandfather's will, so he **set** himself **up** as a photographer.
c. This bad weather's really **getting** me **down**.
d. The flat isn't very nice, but I can **put up with** it until I find somewhere better.
e. The family dog was old and crippled, so they decided reluctantly that they had to have her **put down**.
f. Let's meet on the 20th. **Put** the date **down** in your diary so you don't forget it.
g. James Gregory was **sent down** for ten years for his part in the robbery.
h. Peter thinks I'm trying to **get off with** his girlfriend, but I don't find her very attractive. Anyway, I wouldn't do a thing like that to a mate of mine.

i. Have you seen how Jane is always **putting** him **down**? Either she criticizes him for the way he dresses, or the way he eats or the way he speaks, and she makes him feel such a fool!
j. 'I've been **set up**,' thought Alice. 'Joe told the director that I was incompetent, then altered the accounts making it look like my handwriting, and now I've been accused of stealing money!'
k. Jeremy, who is a very good mimic, was **sending up** the Director and the way he screws up his face when he talks, when the Director himself came into the room. You could have heard a pin drop!

2 Match the multi-word verbs above with one of the following definitions.

_____ to depress, make miserable

_____ to send to prison

_____ to establish a business

_____ to provide a bed for someone for a short while

_____ to imitate someone in such a way as to make them appear foolish

_____ to write down

_____ to kill (an animal) out of humanitarian reasons

_____ to tolerate

_____ to begin a romantic or sexual relationship with someone

_____ to make someone appear guilty in order to get them into trouble

_____ to make someone seem foolish by criticizing and ridiculing them

Reading

Now read the article.
1 In what way does the 'teacher' make fun of . . .
- political pollsters?
- Val Doonican (an entertainer with a certain popular appeal)?
- mothers-in-law?
- the police?
- American English?
2 What is the student's confusion at the end of the 'lesson'?
3 Which multi-word verbs does the 'teacher' explain well, and which badly?

MILES KINGTON

Learning English as a Second Language

Part 597: Dealing with political pollsters.

Please help me. What do I say if I am stopped in the street by a man asking questions about elections? This was happening to me all the time during the general election.

You say: "Put me down as a Don't Know".

Put me down as a Don't Know. I see. What exactly does that mean?

It means you don't want any more questions.

I see. What does "put me down" mean?

It means, write me down on paper.

But in Lesson 413, you told me that "put down" means to make a lot of fun of. Your sentence was "Every comedian thinks it is funny to put down Val Doonican."

Yes, well, it means that as well.

So maybe the man asking the questions will make fun of me?

No, no.

And in lesson 512, you said that "put down" also means to have your favourite animal killed. Your sentence was: "We are taking our cat to the vet for him to be put down."

Did I? Well, yes, it means that too.

So I am afraid that the man asking the political questions will have me painlessly killed when I say "Put me down as a Don't Know."

No, no, he won't do that. I promise.

If "put down" means to make fun of, I suppose "put up" means to take seriously.

No, no. It means to accommodate for a few days. Here is another sentence for you: "My mother has written

Could I say to the vet, 'Here is my cat, please have her sent up?'

to say she is coming to stay with us, so we will have to put her up for the weekend."

That is a bit like a sentence I remember from lesson 87. "I do my best to put up with your mother."

Ah, yes, that's put up with.

What does "put down with mean?"

Nothing.

Could I say "Set me down as a Don't Know"?

No. "Set down" means to let someone off a train at a railway station.

And "set up" means to let them on the train at the railway station?

Mmm, not exactly. Actually, it means something the police do when all else fails. Here is another sentence for you. "I spent three years in jail because the police set me up for the Croydon job".

Would they do that?

Not if you'd really done the Croydon job. "Set up," by the way, also means to give someone lots of money. For example, my parents set me up as a teacher of English as a second language.

But the police would not give you lots of money for the Croydon job?

No, I think not.

Would it be possible to say to this man in the street: "Send me down as a Don't Know?

Well, not really, "Send down" means to put someone in prison.

Oh, I see. The police set you up first and then they send you down.

Yes. Well, not quite. The police set you up, but the judges send you down.

This is all done to make more jobs?

Yes, I think so.

Well, if "send down" means to put you in prison, does "send up" mean get someone out of prison?

Not exactly. In fact, not at all. "Send up" means to make a lot of fun of.

Ah, just like "put down". So the sentence from lesson 413 could also be: "Every comedian thinks it is funny to send up Val Doonican"?

Very good, absolutely right. Spot on.

And I could also say to the man in the street: "Send me up as a Don't Know".

No.

And I could say to the vet: "Here is my cat — please have her sent up"?

No.

English is very difficult to learn as a second language.

Believe me, English is very difficult to *teach* as a second language. It gets me down sometimes.

Get down? You mean, as in the phrase: "Get down and boogie"?

Where did you learn to speak like that?

In a disco in the West End, where I also learn English as a second language.

Ah, no, that is American as a second language. Oh, just look at the time. I think that is enough for today's lesson. I must get off.

Get off with whom?

I will deal with that in our next lesson.

After reading

What are some of the problems of multi-word verbs illustrated in the article?

There is an exercise on multi-word verbs in every other unit of the Workbook (Units 2, 4, 6, etc.).

UNIT 2

1 'The Picture of Dorian Gray'

The following are extracts from *The Picture of Dorian Gray*. Put the verb in brackets in the appropriate tense.

The tenses used are Past Simple and Continuous, Past Perfect, and **would** to express the future in the past.

When you have finished, look at page 26 of the Student's Book to check your answers.

As he (a) _____ (turn) the handle of the door,

his eye (b) _____ (fall) upon the portrait Basil

Hallward (c) _____ (paint) of him. He

(d) _____ (start) back as if in surprise. Then he

(e) _____ (go) on into his own room, looking

somewhat puzzled. After he (f) _____ (take)

the buttonhole out of his coat, he (g) _____ (seem) to hesitate.

He (h) _____ (throw) himself into a chair, and began to think. Suddenly there flashed across his mind

what he (i) _____ (say) in Basil Hallward's

studio the day the picture (j) _____ (finish).

Yes, he (k) _____ (remember) it perfectly. He

(l) _____ (utter) a mad wish that he himself might remain young, and the portrait grow old . . .

Surely his wish (m) _____ (not fulfil)?

But this murder — was it to dog him all his life? Was he always to be burdened by his past? Was he really to confess? Never. There was only one bit of evidence left against him. The picture itself — that was evidence. He (a) _____ (destroy) it. Why

(b) _____ he _____ (keep) it so long?

Once it (c) _____ (give) him pleasure to watch it changing and growing old. Of late it (d) _____

(give) him no such pleasure. It (e) _____ (keep) him awake at night.

He (f) _____ (look) around, and (g) _____

(see) the knife that (h) _____ (stab) Basil

Hallward. He (i) _____ (clean) it many times,

till there was no stain left upon it. It (j) _____

(be) bright, and glistened. As it (k) _____

(kill) the painter, so it (l) _____ (kill) the painter's work, and all that that meant.

When they (m) _____ (enter), they

(n) _____ (find), hanging upon the wall, a

splendid portrait of their master as they (o) _____ last (see) him, in all the wonder of his exquisite youth and beauty. Lying on the floor was a dead man, in evening dress, with a knife in his heart . . . It was not

until they (p) _____ (examine) the rings that

they (q) _____ (recognize) who it

(r) _____ (be).

2 The future in the past

Was/were going to and the Past Continuous are quite commonly used to express the future as seen from a point in the past.

*We **were going to** play tennis, but it started to rain. She was in a hurry, because she **was meeting** her publisher.*

Would is rare in this use, but is common in indirect speech and thought.

*He said he **would** come.*
*I thought he **would** win.*

To understand the difference between these three forms, it helps to put them into their real future form.

*We're **going to** play tennis.* (Intention)
*She's **meeting** her publisher.* (Arrangement)
'I'll come,' he said. (Spontaneous intention)
'He'll win, I'm sure,' I thought. (Prediction)

Practice

Put the verb in brackets in an appropriate form to express future in the past.

a. Henry! Good Lord! I forgot you _____ (come) for supper. I haven't bought anything to eat at all! Never mind. Come in.

b. The police _____ (charge) me with robbery, but I finally managed to persuade them that they had the wrong person.

c. The start of the film was dreadful. I hoped it

_____ (get) better, but in fact it got worse as it went on.

d. I went to bed early as I _____ (leave) for New York the next day, and I wanted to feel refreshed when I arrived.

e. She didn't worry about her son, Tom. He was a

sensible boy, and she knew he _____ (take) care of himself.

f. **A** Did I tell you about the wedding?
   B No. You _____ (show) me the photos, but we were interrupted.

g. Our last holiday was disastrous. We _____ (go) away to Austria, but I broke my arm, so we couldn't drive, and the children got the measles, so we had to cancel it at the last moment.

h. I _____ just _____ (ring) the receptionist to say that I couldn't get the television to work in my hotel room when the engineer arrived to fix it.

i. I had invited Pat and Peter for supper at 8.00, but I didn't start getting things ready until 7.30 because

I knew they _____ (be) late. They always were.

j. Aren't you Annie Beecroft? Do you remember me?

Last time I saw you, you _____ (emigrate) to Canada! Did you?

3 Past Simple, 'used to', and 'would' for past habits

Used to can be used to express past habits and states.
*We **used to** go out a lot.* (habit)
*He **used to** be very short-tempered.* (state)

Would can express typical behaviour. Whereas **used to** is quite factual, **would** looks at past habits rather nostalgically.

*We had some lovely holidays by the sea when I was young. We'**d** spend the day collecting sea-shells, or we'**d** go for long walks on the cliffs.*

Would cannot be used to express past states. (We cannot say **He'd live in a lovely cottage.*) If the past action happened only once (and is therefore not a habit), the Past Simple must be used.

Practice

Read the following story. Which of the verbs in italics
1 can change to **would** or **used to**?
2 can change only to **used to**?
3 must stay in the Past Simple?

We (a) *met* while we were doing a course in London. It wasn't exactly love at first sight, but I often (b) *found* myself looking in his direction, and he always (c) *smiled* back, and his eyes (d) *lingered* just a little longer than was necessary. So we (e) *started* having lunch together in a small cafe, and then, if the weather was fine, we (f) *went* for a walk in the park, and (g) *chatted* endlessly about everything. He (h) *lived* at one end of town, and I was miles away, but we often (l) *met* at weekends. I (j) *thought* it would last for ever, but of course it didn't. Nothing does!

Write some sentences about what you did when you were a child using the verb forms to express past actions and habits.

4 The spelling of regular verb forms

help¹ /help/ v 1

The dictionary gives no information about spelling when the verb is completely regular.

rub¹ /rʌb/ v (-bb-)

Many regular verbs double the final consonant to make other verb forms. The dictionary entry tells us this.

From these entries, we know the following information.

Infinitive	Past tense/ past participle	Present participle
help	helped	helping
rub	rubbed	rubbing

Use your dictionary to complete the following charts, paying attention to spelling.

Infinitive	Past tense/ past participle	Present participle
hop		
slam		
plot		
stab		
ban		

Can you work out the rule? Why do we write **stopped**, but not *cleanned or *keepping?

prefer		
permit		
refer		
admit		
enter		
benefit		
develop		

Can you work out the rule? Why are the last three different? Why don't we write *visitted?

travel		
quarrel		
cancel		

What do you notice about the difference between British and American spelling?

Writing

5 'At the beginning', 'In the end', etc.

The words and expressions that tell us when something happens in a story are not all used in quite the same way.

At the beginning (of the story) tells us the chronological point.
In the beginning and **at first** suggest a contrast later. We expect to hear **but later** the circumstances changed.

At the end (of the story) tells us the chronological point.
In the end suggests a contrast earlier. Before, there were problems and uncertainty.

Finally and **eventually** suggest a long wait. (**Finally** usually comes before the verb.) The outcome may be positive or negative.
At last suggests a very long wait. The outcome is positive.

Practice 1

Compare the following pairs of sentences.

a. John and Anita got married **at the beginning of May**.
   In the beginning, the marriage worked well, but problems soon began to emerge.
b. **At the end of the war**, the soldiers all went home.
   We had a long and bitter argument, but **in the end** I realized he was right after all.
c. I burnt the meat and dropped the vegetables, but the meal turned out all right **in the end**.
   At last the waiter brought them their meal, but by then it was cold.

Practice 2

Put one of the above words or expressions into each gap.

a. After the operation, he went home to recuperate.

   _____ he made good progress, but his condition soon began to deteriorate.

b. _____ of the film, we are introduced to the two main characters, Bill and Sarah Cunningham.
c. Damian told me the other day that he wants to be

   an astronaut. I didn't believe him _____, but then I realized he was serious!
d. She spent days trying to decide what to do. She

   _____ decided that the best course of action was to do nothing.

e. I've spent thousands of pounds trying to get my driving licence, and now, after seventeen goes, I've got it _____!

f. They tried hard to make the marriage work, but their hearts weren't in it, and they got divorced _____.

g. The story jumps around from place to place, and there are characters introduced who don't seem to be connected. _____, you have very little idea of what it was all about.

h. I had to wait weeks for the cheque to come, but it arrived _____.

Practice 3

Write an appraisal of a book, film or play that you either liked or disliked.

Give some information about the story and the characters, and say why it did or didn't impress you.

Pronunciation

6 Losing a syllable

Sometimes, syllables which are apparent in the spelling of a word are lost (or nearly lost) when they are spoken.

lit~e~rature	Ooo
alt~e~red	Oo
comf~o~rtable	Ooo

In the following words, cross out the syllable which is often lost when spoken, and write the number of the stress pattern after it.

1 Oo
2 Ooo
3 oOo
4 oOoo

remembered	____
passionately	____
moderately	____
wizened	____
murmured	____
quivering	____
enamoured	____
deepened	____
scandalous	____
glistening	____
considerably	____
burdened	____
different	

Vocabulary

7 Gap filling – an extract from Charlie Chaplin's autobiography

Put one suitable word into each gap.

I remember standing in the wings when Mother's voice cracked and went into a whisper. The audience began to laugh and sing falsetto and to make catcalls. It was all vague and I did not quite understand what was going on. But the noise increased until Mother was (a) _____ to walk off the stage. When she came into the wings she was very upset and argued with the stage manager who, having seen me (b) _____ before Mother's friends, said something about letting me go on in her (c) _____ .

And in the (d) _____ I remember him leading me by the hand and, after a few explanatory words to the audience, leaving me on the stage alone. And before a (e) _____ of footlights and faces and smoke, I started to sing, (f) _____ by the orchestra, which fiddled about until it found my (g) _____ . It was a well-known song called *Jack Jones*.

Half-way through, a shower of money (h) _____ on to the stage. Immediately I stopped and (i) _____ that I would pick up the money first and sing (j) _____ . This caused much laughter. The stage manager came on with a handkerchief and helped me to (k) _____ it up. I thought he was going to keep it. This thought was conveyed to the audience and increased their laughter especially when he walked off with it with me (l) _____ following him. Not until he handed it to Mother did I return and continue to sing. I was quite at (m) _____ . I talked to the audience, danced and did several imitations including one of Mother singing her Irish march song.

And in repeating the chorus, in all innocence I imitated Mother's voice cracking and was surprised at the (n) _____ it had on the audience. There was laughter and cheers, then more money-throwing; and when Mother came on the stage to carry me off, her presence evoked tremendous applause. That night was my first (o) _____ on the stage and Mother's last.

8 The four types

There are four types of multi-word verbs.

Type 1 — verb + adverb (no object)
*The plane **took off**.*
*The fire **went out**.*
*Our plans **fell through**.*

Type 2 — verb + adverb + object
*Could you **hand out** the books/**hand** the books **out**?*
*Could you **hand** them **out**?*
*We'll have to **put off** the meeting/**put** the meeting **off**.*
*We'll have to **put** it **off**.*
The adverb can change position, but not if the object is a pronoun.

Type 3 — verb + preposition + object
*He **ran across** the road.*
*She **takes after** her mother.*
*He **came into** a lot of money when his father died.*
The preposition cannot change position.

Type 4 — verb + adverb + preposition + object
*She **looks down on** working-class people.*
*I'm sorry to **break in on** your conversation.*
*Please **get on with** your work.*

Notice how the dictionary entry gives literal meanings first, then non-literal meanings, and tells you which type of multi-word verb it is.

> **break up** (**a**) (of members of a group) go away in different directions; disperse: *The meeting broke up at eleven o'clock.* (**b**) (*Brit*) (of a school, its staff or its pupils) begin the holidays when school closes at the end of term: *When do you break up for Christmas?* (**c**) become very weak; collapse: *He was breaking up under the strain.* (**d**) (esp of a period of fine weather) end: *The weather shows signs of breaking up.* **break** (**sth**) **up** (**a**) (cause sth to) separate into smaller pieces by cutting, striking, etc: *The ship broke up on the rocks.* ○ *The ship was broken up for scrap metal.* (**b**) (cause to) come to an end: *Their marriage is breaking up.* ○ *They decided to break up the partnership.* **break sth up** (**a**) disperse or scatter sth using force: *Police were called in to break up the meeting.* (**b**) divide sth by means of analysis, an administrative decision, etc: *Sentences can be broken up into clauses.* ○ *The government has broken up the large private estates.* **break up** (**with sb**) end a relationship with sb: *She's just broken up with her boyfriend.*

Break up is type 1 — there is no **sb** (somebody) or **sth** (something).
Definition **a** is literal; definitions **b**, **c** and **d** are more metaphorical.

Break something up is type 2 — the position of **sth** before the adverb tells you that the adverb can change position.

> **take to sb/ sth** develop a liking for sb/sth; develop an ability for sth: *I didn't take to her husband at all.* ○ *I took to her the moment I met her.* ○ *He hasn't taken to his new school.*

Take to something is type 3 — the position of **sth** after the preposition tells you that it cannot change position.

> **get 'through (to sb)** (**a**) reach (sb): *Thousands of refugees will die if these supplies don't get through (to them).* (**b**) make contact (with sb), esp by telephone: *I tried ringing you several times yesterday but I couldn't get through (to you).*

Get through (to somebody) can either be type 1 or type 4.

> **get away with sth** (**a**) steal sth and escape with it: *Thieves raided the bank and got away with a lot of money.* (**b**) receive (a relatively light punishment): *For such a serious offence he was lucky to get away with a fine.*

Get away with something is type 4.

Type 2 is the most common form of multi-word verb.

Practice

Here are five more dictionary entries. After each one there are four sentences. Two of these sentences use the multi-word verb correctly; in the other two, however, there is one mistake of form and one of meaning. Identify the two correct sentences.

> **let sb off** (**with sth**) not punish sb (severely): *She was let off with a fine instead of being sent to prison.* ○ *Don't let these criminals off lightly,* ie Punish them severely. **let sb off** (**sth**) not compel sb to do (sth): *We've been let off school today because our teacher is ill.*

a. You shouldn't have lied to me. I'll let you off this time, but don't do it again.
b. James stole ten pounds, but the judge let off him as he had a family to support.
c. The teacher let his class off homework because he felt in a good mood.
d. Joe badly needed money, so we let him off with a cheque.

> **get
> round sb** (also **get around sb**) (*infml*) persuade
> sb to agree to sth or to do sth which he first
> opposed: *She knows how to get round her father.*

e. He didn't want to lend me his car, but I got round him by offering to fill it up with petrol.

f. Annie couldn't do her homework, so I got round her and soon it was finished.

g. My wife wanted to go to America for our holiday, and I wanted to go to Italy, but she got me round in the end.

h. I try to put my foot down as a parent, but my daughter always manages to get round me somehow.

> **back out (of sth)** withdraw from (an agreement, promise, etc): *It's too late to back out (of the deal) now.*

i. I backed twenty pounds out of the bank.

j. Sir Malcolm Saunders offered to buy the company, but he backed out when he heard it was heavily in debt.

k. What do you mean, you've changed your mind? It's our wedding today! You can't back out of it now!

l. Once you've given your word, don't try to back it out.

> **3** (phr v) **own up (to sth)**
> (*infml*) admit or confess that one is to blame (for sth): *Nobody owned up to the theft.* ○ *Eventually she owned up.*

m. *Teacher to class*: Nobody is going home until the culprit owns up. Who put glue on my chair?

n. When confronted with the steely eyes of his employer, the butler owned up to stealing the money that had disappeared.

o. He owned to the murder of his wife up.

p. She wrote a postcard home, and owned up to enjoying her holiday immensely.

> **take sth back (a)** (of a shop) agree to accept or receive back (goods previously bought there): *We only take goods back if customers can produce the receipt.* **(b)** admit that sth one said was wrong or that one should not have said it; retract or withdraw sth: *I take back what I said (about you being selfish).* **take sb back (to...)** cause sb's thoughts to return to a past time: *The smell of seaweed took him back to his childhood.* ○ *Hearing those old songs takes me back a bit.*

q. I take back all those horrible things I said about you. You really are an awful person.

r. I decided I didn't like the colour of the dress, so I took back it to the shop.

s. The smell of porridge took me back to the days when, as a boy, I used to stay in youth hostels while on walking holidays.

t. How dare you call me a cheat! Take that back immediately!

UNIT 3

1 'As' or 'like'?

Complete the following sentences with **as** or **like**.

a. _____ a boy, I used to like going for long walks in the early morning.

b. Some adults behave just _____ children when they don't get their own way.

c. My daughters' favourite game is to dress up

_____ nurses and play hospitals.

d. They use a pencil _____ a thermometer, and take the temperature of all their teddy bears.

e. I'm a very fussy person, who wants everything to

be in its right place. I'm _____ you in that way.

f. But I'm not intolerant of other people,

_____ you are.

g. In America, _____ in Europe, unemployment is a growing problem.

h. Andy drinks _____ a fish! I've never seen anyone drink so much.

i. My sister was always seen _____ the black sheep of the family.

j. When she was young, she never wore dresses because she wanted to look _____ a boy.

k. I met someone today who went to the same

school _____ I did.

l. _____ me, he became a teacher, and then began to write.

m. He's just got a job _____ director of a small company.

2 'As . . . as' for comparison

Change the structure of the following sentences, but without changing their meaning. Use **as . . . as** or **not as/so . . . as**. Each sentence has been begun for you.

a. Our children behave much better than theirs.

Their children _____

_____

b. Their house has a larger garden than ours.

Our garden _____

_____

c. What I earn in a month, he earns in a week.

He earns _____

d. I expected the food they served to be nicer than it was.

The food _____

_____

e. Henry had more champagne than me.

I _____

_____

f. But I had more mussels than anybody else.

Nobody had _____

_____

g. The party ended earlier than I thought it would.

The party didn't go on _____

h. Fewer people came to the party than he anticipated.

There weren't _____

_____

18

i. Sheila usually behaves dreadfully, but she didn't this time.

Sheila didn't _____

_____

j. She usually wears a lot of jewellery, but she didn't tonight.

She didn't _____

_____

k. I see less of her than I used to.

I don't see _____

_____

l. We enjoyed the evening more than the children.

The children _____

_____

3 Constructions with the 'as . . . as' pattern

Complete the following sentences in an appropriate way.

a. Reports are coming into the news desk of a train crash in southern Scotland. As many as

_____ .

b. Some restaurants have a fixed price, no matter how much you have to eat. At 'The Carvery', for instance, you can _____ for just £7.50.

c. I used to be able to get to work in an hour. Now it takes me two hours. So it takes me twice

_____ .

d. David's got more money than sense. As well as his house in London, _____

_____ .

e. The city is a bit dangerous at night, but you'll be perfectly safe as long as _____ .

f. Yes, I think Wednesday would be a good day for you to come. As far as I remember, _____

_____ .

4 Comparing statistics

Look at the charts of two people's monthly expenditure, and make sentences.

John spends twice as much on food as he used to. he did last year.
David spends 50% more on food than John does.

David spends nearly three times as much on transport as John does.

EXPENDITURE PER MONTH

		Last year	Now
John	Food	£100	£200
	Transport	£ 40	£120
	Entertainment	£100	£150
	Accommodation	£200	£200
	Salary	£500	£990

David	Food	£ 300
	Transport	£ 350
	Entertainment	£ 900
	Accommodation	£1000
	Salary	£3000

_____

_____

_____

_____

_____

_____

_____

_____

_____

Verb patterns

5 Infinitive or '-ing'?

Complete the sentences using the correct form of the verb in brackets (either the infinitive or the **-ing** form).

The teacher	(a) lets	us	_____	(use) a dictionary.
	(b) allows		_____	
	(c) asks		_____	
	(d) expects		_____	
	(e) makes		_____	

19

I
(f) am thinking of _____
(g) would rather _____
(h) had better _____ (go) home.
(i) don't mind _____
(j) am hoping _____
(k) am helping her _____
I (l) succeeded in _____ (finish) the work as
(m) intend _____ soon as possible.
(n) was made _____

6 Verbs that take the infinitive and '-ing'

Put the verb in brackets in either the infinitive or the -ing form.

a. I used to _____ (think) that life ended at 30.

   I'm not used to _____ (think) so hard this early in the morning.

b. Jane was never a very reliable friend. If I were you, I'd try _____ (forget) her.
   If your clothes don't seem very white after you've washed them, try _____ (soak) them in a little bleach.

c. Please stop _____ (make) such a terrible noise!

   After half an hour, we stopped _____ (make) a cup of tea.

d. I remember _____ (see) him in the part of Hamlet at the Academy Theatre.

   Did you remember _____ (see) Tim and tell him that we can't come on Saturday?

e. I started _____ (read) classical literature at the age of six.

   Oh, look! It's starting _____ (rain).

f. He went on _____ (write) his essay despite the noise.
   The lecture began very badly, but the professor went on _____ (make) some interesting points.

g. I couldn't help them _____ (find) what they were looking for as I was in too much of a hurry.
   Harry looked so funny that I couldn't help

_____ (laugh).

h. I like _____ (pay) bills quite promptly. It's so easy to get behind.

   I like _____ (be) the centre of attention.

i. Do you like _____ (cook)?

   When we have a dinner party, I like

   _____ (cook) something really exotic that nobody's ever had before.

7 Verbs of perception

Verbs of perception, for example, **hear** and **watch**, can be followed by the infinitive without **to** or the -ing form.

*I heard someone **scream**.*
*I watched him **make** a toy aeroplane.*
*I heard someone **screaming**.*
*I watched him **making** a toy aeroplane.*

The infinitive form suggests that the verb action happens once and that the whole action is perceived. The -ing form suggests the verb action goes on for some time, and only part of it is perceived.
Put the verbs in brackets in the infinitive (without to) or the -ing form.

a. I heard my neighbours _____ (turn) off

   their television and _____ (go) to bed.

b. I woke up at two in the morning. I could hear my

   neighbours _____ (have) an argument.

c. When I looked through the window, I saw her

   _____ (read) a book.

d. When she saw me _____ (come), she waved.

e. She could feel her heart _____ (pound) as she neared the end of the race.

f. Can you smell something _____ (burn)?

g. When I came into the room, I saw her _____ (lean) casually against the fireplace.

h. It was obvious that she hadn't heard me

   _____ (come) in. I saw her _____

   (go) over to the drawer and _____ (take) out a gun.

i. I've never seen anyone _____ (eat) as much as you do.

j. As I woke up, I could hear my mother downstairs

   _____ (make) breakfast.

Future forms

8 Producing the correct form

Put the verb in brackets in a suitable future form. Sometimes more than one form is possible.

John and Anita (a) _____ (get) married in two

weeks' time. The church ceremony (b) _____

(start) at 3.00, so all the guests (c) _____
(have) to be in their seats by 2.50. Anita

(d) _____ (give) away by her brother, as her
father died a few years ago, and John's brother, Paul,

(e) _____ (be) his best man, so he

(f) _____ (have) to make sure all the

arrangements go smoothly. They (g) _____
(have) the reception in the King's Head Hotel, and then

the happy couple (h) _____ (go) to Italy for

their honeymoon. They (i) _____ (stay) in a
hotel near Lake Como for two weeks, and when they

come back Anita (j) _____ (start) looking for

a job. By the time it's all over, it (k) _____
(cost) them over two thousand pounds! What a lot of
money!

A When (l) _____ you _____ (get)

changed? The taxi (m) _____ (arrive) any
minute, and you aren't even ready yet!

B Don't worry. We've got ages. What time

(n) _____ the play _____ (start)?
7.00, isn't it? If the traffic isn't too bad, we

(o) _____ (get) to the theatre by 6.30, and

then we (p) _____ (have) time for a quick
drink.

A What (q) _____ we _____ (do)
about eating tonight?

B Keith (r) _____ (take) us out to a Chinese
restaurant afterwards. Had you forgotten?

A Oh, yes. What time (s) _____ we

_____ (get) back? I (t) _____ (have)
to tell the babysitter.

B About midnight, I should think.

9 Future forms – shades of meaning

Underline the future form which is most appropriate.

a. So you've sold your house? When **will you move/will you be moving**?
b. Darling, I love you. **Are you going to/will you** marry me?
c. I hear you've been offered a new job. **Do you/are you going to** accept it or not?
d. Do you think they **will find/will have found** a way to stop people ageing by the time we're old?
e. Yes, I'm sure one **will have been found/will be found** soon.
f. Hurry up and buy your ticket. The train **will leave/will be leaving** soon, and I don't want to miss it.
g. Which platform **will it/does it** leave from?
h. I forgot to ask a neighbour to look after the plants while we're away on holiday! When we get home, they **will all have died/will all die**.
i. Damn! We're going to be late for the party. By the time we get there, all the others **will be eating/will have eaten**, and **there'll be/there's going to be** nothing left for us.

Writing

10 Linking cause and result

Study the linking devices in the following sentences.

Links for result

*She worked **so hard**
She did **such** good work* | *(that) she was promoted.*

*He was **too** lazy
He wasn't hard-working
enough* | ***to be** promoted.
for the firm to promote
him.*

*There wasn't **enough** work **for** him to do.*

Links for cause

*I went to bed early **because** I had to get up at six in the morning.*

***As**
Since* | *the weather showed no signs of improving,
the match was called off.*

Because is generally used when the reason is the most important part of the sentence. The **because**-clause usually comes at the end.

As and **since** are used when the reason is already well-known, or is less important than the rest of the sentence. **As**- and **since**-clauses often begin the sentence.

*I had to get up at six in the morning, **so** I went to bed early.*

The government was determined to curb inflation. **Consequently,** / **Therefore,** *there were no pay awards above four per cent.*

Practice 1

Transform the following sentences using the word(s) in brackets, and making any necessary changes.

a. Being an only child, I was often lonely. (because)

_____

b. As I was lonely, my parents bought me a puppy. (so . . . that)

_____

c. She was in a hurry, so she forgot her season ticket. (such . . . that)

_____

d. I only had six driving lessons, so I failed my test. (enough)

_____

e. He didn't go back to work, because he still didn't feel well. (as)

_____

f. I could never be a teacher, because I'm not patient enough. (too)

_____

g. Her performance with the company was so disappointing that she didn't get the promotion she was seeking. (consequently)

_____

h. The car was so expensive that we couldn't afford it. (too)

_____

i. They closed the shop early because there weren't many customers. (so . . . that)

_____

j. Your voice is good. You could train to be an opera singer. (enough . . . for)

_____

k. The book affected me profoundly. It changed my whole life. (such . . . that)

_____

Practice 2

Write one of the following letters.

a. A formal letter of complaint

You were expecting a new suite of furniture to be delivered three months ago. You have already paid for it in full. You were given a delivery date and stayed in, but nothing arrived. On the next delivery date, a van arrived with the wrong suite. On the third delivery date, you left a note pinned to the door saying you were at your neighbour's, but the delivery man didn't read the note and drove away.

The firm's name and address is:
Derwent Furnishings, Ambleside Road,
Preston, Lancashire, BF6 5QL.

b. An informal letter

Write an informal letter to a friend, apologizing and giving reasons for not being able to attend their wedding.

Pronunciation

11 Sentence stress

In the following dialogues, mark where the main stress is in B's replies.

a. **A** It was a nice film, wasn't it?
    B You didn't really like it, did you? I thought it was awful.

b. **A** Thank you for the meal.
    B You didn't really like it, did you? You didn't eat much.

c. **A** What did you think of the film?
    B I liked the scenery, but the acting was poor.

d. **A** Who did you tell about the party?
    B I told Peter.

e. **A** I lost all my money playing cards.
    B I told you.

f. **A** Who told Alice that I've been sacked?
    B I told her.
g. **A** Just think! If you get this job, we'll be able to afford a new car!
    B If I get the job.
h. **A** I've invited Robert Redford round for a drink.
    B Not the Robert Redford!
i. **A** Did you pay the gas bill?
    B I thought you'd paid it!
j. **A** Are you going to pay the bill, or shall I?
    B It doesn't matter who pays it as long as one of us does.
k. **A** This is yours, and you must keep it for ever.
    B I wouldn't give it to anyone.
l. **A** It was very kind of you to give Toby that antique vase.
    B I wouldn't give it to just anyone.

Vocabulary

12 Crossword puzzle

Here is an English crossword for you to try!

Sometimes, the first letter of the answer has been given to help you.

ACROSS

6 A prestigious possession, something people own to show how wealthy they are (6,6)
8 You are in this if you are in a difficult situation and you have to choose between two alternatives (7)
9 Item of furniture (5)
10 Female pigs, or plants seeds! (4)
12 We can say that a person who knows a lot about something is well v----- in it (6)
14 Started (5)
15 Steering device on a boat (6)
16 Information, facts, perhaps from a computer (4)
19 Mistake (5)
21 An action which breaks the laws of God (3)
22 If you have this, you have the strength and stamina to keep going until you reach the end of what you're doing (7,5)

DOWN

1 A religious word meaning regarded as holy (8)
2 A model in a shop window, or a baby's comforter (5)
3 Written composition (5)
4 An informal word which means a great many (7)
5 Explosive device (4)
6 Minor road in a town (4,5)
7 A man who is in charge of a school (10)
11 An income of £10,000 --- year (3)
12 Kind of Commercial vehicle (3)
13 Kinds of bird, or makes food go down your throat (8)
14 Is disloyal to a friend (7)
17 Employing (5)
18 Incompetent (5)
20 Rodents (4)

13 Idioms — key words

In the following sentences, there is an idiom in bold. Decide what you think is the key word, then look in your dictionary to see if you are right. Rewrite the sentences in non-idiomatic English.

a. Don't believe what he said about Trish. He was **talking through his hat**. He doesn't even know her.
b. Come here! I've **got a bone to pick with you**! Why did you tell Anne about Ken and me splitting up? I told you not to tell anyone.
c. I don't think correct spelling is terribly important, but my teacher has a **bee in his bonnet** about it. If we ever make a spelling mistake, he makes us write it out twenty times.
d. **A** I met a man called Anthony Trollope.
    B Mmm. The name **rings a bell**, but I can't put a face to it.
e. Ford Motors have a new saloon car **in the pipeline**, and it will be revealed for the first time at next year's Motor Show.
f. **A** Come on, John! who's right, me or Peter?
    B Don't ask me to decide. I'm **sitting on the fence**.

g. **A** Why did you tell that joke about how mean the Scots are? Didn't you realize that Jimmy is Scottish?

   B No, I didn't. **I put my foot in it**, didn't I?

h. You have to be careful with sales people. They have the **gift of the gab**. Suddenly you can find you've bought something that you really didn't want.

i. **A** This morning when I was on the train, I had to stand because it was crowded. Suddenly, the door flew open while we were moving.

   B How did you save yourself?

   A A man grabbed hold of me and pulled me in.

   B That was **a close shave!**

j. The company has put forward many reasons why it can't offer a substantial pay rise. The reason, **in a nutshell**, is that the company is very nearly bankrupt.

14 Dependent prepositions

Write the correct preposition in each gap.

To join or not to join?

At no point in my life have I been keen (a) _____ the idea of joining any kind of club or group. I rebelled (b) _____ it (c) _____ a very early age, when my mother tried to force me

(d) _____ becoming a member of the Girl Guides. I went once, or at least, I got as far as looking in the door of the church hall, but I couldn't

cope (e) _____ the sight of all those confident-looking girls in blue, competing so heartily

(f) _____ each other (g) _____ all those games and activities, so I ran home

(h) _____ tears. My mother despaired

(i) _____ me, but persisted (j) _____ her attempts to get me to join something. She was

keen (k) _____ me to go to ballet classes. I actually got in through the door this time, and

(l) _____ the whole this was more successful

than the guides. I emerged (m) _____ my first

lesson, eyes shining with the dream (n) _____ being a prima ballerina. Unfortunately I had not

reckoned (o) _____ being totally lacking

(p) _____ talent, so my enthusiasm

(q) _____ ballet lasted a little less than a year. Later in life I puzzled over my friends' desire to join tennis clubs, bridge clubs, Young Wives Clubs, Old Wives Clubs, pottery classes and the like. They

pleaded (r) _____ me to go with them, but I couldn't bear to. Such clubs didn't interest me

(s) _____ the slightest. Why am I so allergic

(t) _____ groups? I don't suffer

(u) _____ shyness. I can't really understand it.

Perhaps the key (v) _____ my problem lies in the fact that I'm an only child. I just don't know.

UNIT 4

1 Expressing probability

Write **will**, **won't**, **must**, **can't**, or **should**, and an appropriate infinitive (present or past, simple or continuous) in each gap. Change the verb in brackets as necessary.

OK. Don't worry about the phone. I'll answer it. It

(a) _____ (be) David ringing me about tonight's meeting.
'Hello. 37885.'
'Hello John. It's David. I tried ringing you earlier,

but I got no reply. You (b) _____ (be) out.'

'I haven't been out all morning. You (c) _____ (get) the right number.
Never mind. What about the meeting? How many people can we expect?'

'There (d) _____ (be) quite a few, judging by the number of enquiries we've been having. One thing's worrying me. I haven't heard from the speaker, Joan Bakewell. I'm sure she

(e) _____ (forget), but it isn't like her not to get in touch. Shall I give her a ring?'

'Not now, no. She (f) _____ (teach). You'd better wait an hour or so.'
'I've bought twenty bottles of wine for the party afterwards. That (g) _____ (be) enough, don't you think?'
'Yes, plenty. I'll see you later, then. Bye.'
'Bye.'

'You (h) _____ (be) very excited about your new book.'

'Yes, I am. It (i) _____ (sell)

quite well if the publishers' research is accurate.'
'It (j) _____ (take) you a long time to write.'
'About three years, yes.'
'What about your first book?'

'I'm not terribly sure, but it (k) _____ (do) very well, because it hasn't been reprinted, and the first print run was only five hundred copies.'
'Better luck with this one!'
'Thanks!'

'My bank statement says I'm overdrawn. There

(l) _____ (be) some mistake. I

(m) _____ (get) through a whole month's salary already!'

'We (n) _____ (spend) too much money on the house lately.'
'But how come I'm overdrawn?'

'It (o) _____ (be) the desk we bought. It was over eight hundred pounds.'
'How much have you got?'
'About four hundred pounds.'

'Oh, well. That (p) _____ (get) us through to the end of the month if we're careful.'

'Do you think Joey (q) _____ (get) my letter yet?'

'She (r) _____ (receive) it by now. I haven't heard of any hold-ups with the post. When did you send it?'
'Last week. I just wonder why she hasn't rung to tell us how she intends to pay us back the money she owes us.'

'She (s) _____ (think) up a good excuse as to why she can't, I bet.'

25

2 Expressing possibility

Write **may**, **might**, or **could** with an appropriate infinitive (present or past, simple or continuous) in each gap. Often all three are possible, but pay attention to the form of the infinitive.

I wonder why Alan didn't buy me anything for my birthday. I suppose he (a) _____ (forget). Or he (b) _____ (think) that now I'm getting on, I don't like to be reminded of my advancing years. On the other hand, he

(c) _____ (not forget)! He

(d) _____ (give) me a present this evening when I see him. Oh no! He

(e) _____ (plan) a surprise party, as he did last year. What a disaster that was! I hope he isn't doing it again!

Every time I phone Jane, it's engaged. It's very annoying. I suppose she (f) _____ (try) to phone me while I'm phoning her. I'll wait a while.

I can't help worrying when Jack is late back home.

I always think that he (g) _____ (have) an accident, and that he (h) _____ (lie) on the side of the road with ambulances and police cars all about him. I know it's irrational. Wait a minute! It's Tuesday today, isn't it?

He works late some Tuesdays. He (i) _____ (not leave) the office yet. I'll give him a ring.

I wonder why Helen has got all these books on Greece from the library. I suppose she (j) _____ (think) of going there on holiday.

On the other hand, she (k) _____ (not get) them out for herself. They (l) _____ (be) for Henry. He (m) _____ (write) a project on Greece for his geography course.

3 Expressing ability

Write **could**, **managed to** or an appropriate form of **able to** in each gap.

a. What's forty-eight divided by eight? I _____ never _____ to do sums in my head.

b. _____ drive has changed my whole life. Now I can go wherever I want without having to worry about public transport.

c. I had a row with Sheila last night about nuclear arms. I _____ understand the point she was trying to make, but I still didn't agree.

d. A girl was drowning, but I jumped in and I _____ save her. I _____ swim since I was six.

e. The view was breathtaking. You _____ see right across the valley to the hills in the distance.

f. Why don't you stop smoking? You _____ do it if you tried.

g. Anna's operation was very successful. The doctors say she _____ walk again in a few weeks.

h. I'm learning Russian because I want _____ talk to people when I go there next year.

4 Expressing obligation

Write **must**, **need**, or a form of **have to** in each gap. Question forms and negatives are also included.

a. 'What time _____ we _____ leave for the airport?'

'It's only a thirty-minute drive, so we _____ go until about 3.30. I _____ do my packing. I haven't started yet!'

b. I have an interview for a job next week, but before the interview I _____ have a medical examination.

c. How did you damage your bike? You _____ learn to look after your toys. When I was your age, I _____ clean my bike every night.

d. There's a new Indian restaurant just opened that

you _____ go to. It's wonderful! You _____ book, though, because it's so popular already.

e. I'm sure she didn't mean to upset you. You

_____ take things so personally.

f. I hate _____ get up on cold, winter mornings.

g. I hate _____ tell you this, but you've just got a parking ticket.

h. I have perfect teeth. I _____ never _____ have a single filling.

i. I think I've put on weight. I _____ watch what I eat in future.

j. I don't think a career in the army would suit me.

I _____ wear a uniform, for a start.

k. You _____ worry about me. I can look after myself.

l. The doctor said I've got conjunctivitis. I _____ put drops in my eye three times a day.

m. What a wonderful meal that was! You _____ gone to so much trouble!

n. I got something for my cough from the chemists's,

so I _____ go to the doctor's.

o. I was very concerned about how my daughter would find going to her new school, but I

_____ worried, because she loved every minute.

p. You _____ take out travel insurance, but it's a good idea, just to be on the safe side.

5 'Will' and 'would' to express characteristic behaviour

Both **will** and **would** are used to express characteristic behaviour. In this use, they are unstressed.

He'll sit for hours, staring into the fire
My aunt loved writing letters. She'd write twenty or thirty a week.

If the speaker finds the behaviour annoying, **will** and **would** are stressed, and are not contracted.

She will keep interrupting me when I'm trying to concentrate.
He would ask the most stupid questions.

Rewrite the following sentences using **will** or **would**. If the sentence seems to express annoyance, underline the modal verb to show it is stressed.

a. My dog followed me round wherever I went.

_____

b. But he left his hairs on all the furniture.

_____

c. So I had to spend hours trying to get them off.

_____

d. When we went out for a walk, he ran miles and miles.

_____

e. My flatmate adores tea. She drinks six cups at breakfast.

_____

f. But she stubs out her cigarettes in the saucer.

_____

g. My father's quite a wealthy man, but he goes out without any money.

_____

h. He borrows some from whoever's around, but he always pays it back.

_____

Reply questions

6 Reply questions in conversation

Write the correct auxiliary to form questions, tag questions, or reply questions.

A I've had a lovely evening, dear. (a) _____ you?

B Wonderful. The play was marvellous, (b)

_____ it? It had such a surprising ending,

(c) _____ it?

A Mm. And I thought Robert McFarland was very good. But he's aged so much. He didn't use to look so old, (d) _____ he?

B You're right. He's got a lot of grey hair now,

(e) _____ he? I've heard he's been having a few problems recently.

A (f) _____ he?
B Yes. He has a drink problem.

A (g) _____ he?
B Yes. Didn't you see his hand shaking?

A (h) _____ it? Goodness! I didn't notice.
B And before the fight scene, he'd forgotten some of his lines.

A (i) _____ he? You don't miss anything,

(j) _____ you?

B By the way, would you like another drink?

A Be careful, dear, (k) _____ you? You're driving, remember?

B OK. Let's go home, (l) _____ we?

A Good idea.

Writing

7 Linking words and phrases to indicate similarity and comparison

Practice 1

Complete the following sentences appropriately.

a. Only one hundred years ago it took at least five days to cross the Atlantic, **whereas**

_____

b. Increased ease of travel has led to people becoming **more** tolerant of each other's cultures **than**

_____

c. **Besides** being relatively cheap, package holidays

_____

d. My sister and her family always opt for the ease of a package holiday. My family, **on the other hand,**

_____

e. Personally, I dislike being a tourist because one is an observer of another country and its customs without being a part of it. **What is more,** . . .

_____

f. My husband is usually very cautious about trying foreign food. **However,**

_____

g. Both Chinese and Indian cooking incorporate a lot of spices, **but while** the former

_____

h. A charter flight differs from a scheduled flight **in that**

_____

i. **Although** both Brighton and Marbella are seaside resorts, they differ

_____

j. **The more** I see of the world,

_____

Practice 2

Describe the similarities and the differences in meaning between the words in these pairs.

rob − steal
*These words are the same in that they both mean taking property unlawfully. However they differ in that **rob** means to take from a place or a person, for example **to rob a bank**, whereas **steal** means to take an object or article, for example **to steal a watch**.*

to be sacked − to be made redundant
dictionary − encyclopaedia
colleague − accomplice
discussion − argument
typewriter − word processor
excursion − expedition

Practice 3

Write a composition on ONE of the following.

Compare the cuisine of two different countries, or two regions of the same country.
Compare the different newspapers in your country.
Compare the press in your country with the press in Britain.
Compare your language and English.
Compare your experiences of learning English with another subject you have learnt.
Compare the circumstances of your upbringing with those of your parents or grandparents.
Compare your town now with fifty years ago.

Pronunciation

8 Intonation in question tags

There are two kinds of question tag. If the intonation falls, the sentence is more like a statement − 'I'm sure I'm right, confirm this for me.' If the intonation rises, the sentence is more like a real question − 'I think I'm right, but correct me if I'm wrong.' Both are very common in spoken English, as they invite others to comment and join in the conversation.

Decide if the following question tags rise or fall. Put **R** (rise) or **F** (fall) after each one.

a. Lovely day, isn't it? ____

b. You're a clever girl, aren't you? ____

c. You haven't got change for a fiver, have you? ____

d. I'm late, aren't I? Sorry. ____

e. You haven't seen my pen anywhere, have you? ____

f. Let's go home, shall we? __

g. Be careful, dear, won't you? __

h. Give me a hand with this, will you? __

i. You couldn't lend me ten pounds till tomorrow, could you? __

j. You're angry with me, aren't you. I can tell. __

9 How do you pronounce 'ea'?

'ea' in a word is pronounced in several different ways. Put the following words in the correct column according to the pronunciation of '**ea**'. Careful! Three of the words have two different pronunciations (and different meanings)!

scream	spear	knead	bear
bean	break	plead	thread
bread	heal	pear	instead
gear	steak	bead	wear
tear	dead	great	head
breath	yearn	team	year
dread	spread	breathe	mean
lead	read	fear	pearl

10 Words commonly confused

Write sentences to show the difference in meaning between the following pairs or groups of words. Mark the stress, too, as sometimes it shifts.

a. shameful   shameless   ashamed
b. intolerable   intolerant
c. appreciative   appreciable
d. critic   critique
e. confident   confidential
f. disused   misused   unused   abused
g. invaluable   valuable
h. satisfying   satisfactory
i. impressive   impressionable
j. affect   effect
k. moral   morale
l. principal   principle
m. efficient   effective

/e/ (10 words)	/iː/ (11 words)	/eə/ (4 words)	/ɪə/ (5 words)
		/ɜː/ (2 words)	/eɪ/ (3 words)

29

Write one suitable word in each gap.

Give me a real <u>old</u> granny

I was wondering the other day where all the grannies had gone. I don't mean the people who are grannies because they have grandchildren, but the ones who used to be about when I was younger.

I think a granny ought to look a certain way, so that it sticks out a (a) _____ that she is one.

Ideally she should be smallish and round – comfy and cosy. It would be nice if she sat in a (b) _____ chair and crocheted. By a warm fire – a real one – not your posh electric or gas ones with (c) _____ flames and logs.

I think she ought to wear her slippers, and have a canary in a cage, and a window (d) _____ with geraniums. Her hair would be that (e) _____ – white that shows up a pale pink skin and very bright eyes, and she'd smile a lot. I forgot the cat. There should be a cat (f) _____ by the fire. The kettle would always be ready to make a pot of tea, and there would be (g) _____ cakes.

The trouble as I see it is that today's grannies all look wrong. They don't have white hair any more – they have a rinse. They wear make-up and have National Health teeth and go (h) _____ about playing bingo, and don't sit and be cosy anymore.

My grannies would have time to listen to one's (i) _____ and make (j) _____ noises, and when you touched them, they would be soft and yielding, like cushions. The modern ones are all slimline and brittle, and are too busy moving about the place.

I think we should set about seeing if we can't bring back the Old-Time Granny. There's a need for them – they've left a huge (k) _____ in our lives. We can all do with somewhere and somebody we can go to and be 'cosy' every so often.

Still, perhaps nobody but me feels this way. I suppose I'm always thinking backwards instead of forwards, but I'd still like my Old Grannies back again.

It's a (l) _____ thought that I may be a granny myself one day, though. At the moment, I don't (m) _____ sitting and rocking, with a cat or anything else. Or crocheting and making pots of tea and little buns, and smiling all the time and being cosy. I think I would want to head for the great outdoors and the bingo hall, and have my hair and teeth fixed, too.

I suppose, if the experts are right and we're all going to live longer than ever before, my Old Grannies are completely redundant. No, I've just got to (n) _____ the facts, stop going backwards and (o) _____ with the times. I shall try to put the idea out of my mind.

Margaret Cregan

(Evening Standard, 1980)

12 Connections between literal and metaphorical meanings

As you saw in Unit 1, multi-word verbs can have both a literal and a non-literal meaning. Sometimes these can be quite closely related, and if you understand the literal meaning, you can picture the metaphorical meaning.

In the following pairs of sentences, the same multi-word verb is used once literally and once non-literally. Look at the list of verbs below and choose one for each sentence pair. Put the verb into an appropriate form when you fill the gaps.

cover up	**fall back**	**catch up with**
pick up	**pin down**	**wipe out**
sort out	**see through**	**stand up for**

a. My stamp collection was in a terrible mess, so one afternoon I sat down and _____ it _____ according to date and country of origin.

   You and I have a problem of communication, but if we learn to see each other's point of view, I'm sure we can _____ it _____.

b. As he was getting up, he banged his head, and _____ _____ onto the bed with a groan.

   The last years of her life were full of anxiety, and she _____ _____ on her religion to provide succour and support.

c. She had walked ahead of the others, so she stood by a gate and waited for them to _____ _____ _____ her.

   His teachers thought he was bright enough to move up to the next year, and it didn't take him long to _____ _____ _____ his new classmates.

d. Don't let the authorities daunt you. Defend yourself, and _____ _____ _____ your rights!

   The whole theatre audience _____ _____ _____ the Queen's arrival.

e. I didn't learn much Chinese while I was in China on holiday, but I _____ _____ a few useful, everyday phrases.

   Don't just drop the paper on the floor! _____ it _____ and put it in the bin!

f. The house was going to be empty for a long time, so they _____ _____ all the the furniture with dustsheets.

   President Nixon tried to _____ _____ his involvement in the Watergate affair, but the truth came out in the end.

g. The escaping prisoner stumbled and fell, and immediately the police dog jumped on him and _____ him _____ so he couldn't move.

   The plumber has been saying for weeks that he'll come and fix my washing machine, so yesterday I _____ him _____ to a definite date, and he's coming next Tuesday — I hope!

h. The material of her blouse was so fine that you could _____ _____ it.

   He had a superficial charm, but she soon learned to _____ _____ the smooth exterior to the real person underneath.

i. Smallpox has very nearly been _____ _____ in most parts of the world.

   Don't forget to _____ _____ the sink when you've finished the washing up.

UNIT 5

Ways of adding emphasis

1 Emphatic structures

Rewrite the following sentences using, where appropriate, some of the ways of adding emphasis on page 58 of the Student's Book.

a. Tourists are attracted to London because of its sense of history, which they encounter on every street they walk down. London has buildings which date from Roman times, and this makes it such an interesting place to visit.

_____

_____

_____

_____

b. Generally, Londoners welcome the tourists, but normal life is almost impossible at the height of the season, and this is annoying. Tourists drop litter and clog the streets, but they also provide much direct and indirect employment.

_____

_____

_____

_____

c. Having tourists bring so much to the economy is good, but forty million tourists a year isn't.

_____

_____

_____

d. You can always find some new little corner that you haven't come across before, and I like this

about London. The tiny back streets attract me, not the well-publicized tourist spots.

_____

_____

_____

e. Tourists find London noisy and tiring, but they don't realize that the rest of the country is completely different. They have come to see the bright lights of the city, not quiet country lanes.

_____

_____

_____

f. I can't stand the hustle and bustle of the city, and this is why I live in the country. I want peace and quiet more than anything else.

_____

_____

_____

The passive

2 Correcting mistakes

The passive is used when the agent is unknown or unimportant, or when we wish to focus on the object of the active sentence.

My car **was stolen** yesterday.
Houses **are built** using a variety of materials.

'Sunflowers' **was painted** towards the end of Van Gogh's life.

It is also used if we wish to make a statement sound impersonal, perhaps to avoid responsibility when giving bad news, or to sound modest.

Compare the following two sentences that a company might make.

*We **have awarded** our staff a twenty per cent pay rise.*
*Unfortunately, the number of staff **will be reduced** by fifty per cent.*

In the following sentences, some (but not all) of the verbs are in the active where the passive would be more appropriate, and vice versa. Rewrite those which you think need correcting.

a. Someone built this bridge in 1901.
b. No-one has seen the escaped prisoner since a guard was knocked out by him and he ran away.
c. A secretary has invited me to Buckingham Palace to collect an award!
d. Someone wants you in reception.
e. The telephone, which was invented by Alexander Graham Bell in 1876, revolutionized man's ability to communicate.
f. Alexander Graham Bell was a scientist and inventor. The telephone was invented by him in 1876, and he also worked on early radio transmitters.
g. Scientists working in California have discovered a drug which stops premature ageing. They will now manufacture the drug commercially, and it should be available soon.
h. Nobody must take reference books out of the library.
i. The Health Service has prospered under this government. It is true that we have closed hospitals and spent less money, but the system is now streamlined.
j. A tiger was found roaming in a suburban garden today. Mrs Ethel Templeton found the tiger while she was hanging out her washing.
k. We broke a few cups while you were away. Sorry. They'll be replaced. Apart from that, we didn't do much damage at all.
l. I'm a fantastically successful author. I have sold over one million copies of my books.

3 Where is the focus of attention?

Complete the following sentences using the verb in brackets in either the active or the passive, whichever is more appropriate.

a. Yesterday afternoon, the murder trial of James Dent finally came to an end. _____ (sentence) _____.

b. The judge decided to make an example of Mrs Susan Hanson, who had been driving with twice the legal amount of alcohol in her bloodstream.

_____ (sentence) _____.

c. Air hostesses are very busy throughout a flight.

_____ (show) _____ a life jacket,

and _____ (serve) _____.

d. Every attempt is made to make airline passengers feel safe and comfortable. _____ (show)

_____ a lifejacket, _____ (serve)

_____ and _____ (entertain)

_____.

e. Good luck with your new job in Italy. Don't worry about what your duties will be. _____

_____ (tell) _____ when you arrive.

f. Your new boss is Fiorenza di Morno. She's great. Don't worry about what your duties will be.

_____ (tell) _____ when you arrive.

g. I've just had the most gruelling interview.

_____ (ask)_____.

h. One member of the interview panel was really probing. _____ (ask) _____.

i. My father has just retired after working at the same school for thirty years. _____ (give)

_____.

j. Everyone was sorry to see him go, even the pupils. _____ (give) _____.

4 'She is said/thought/considered to be . . .', etc.

Rewrite the following sentences, incorporating the verb of 'thinking' or 'saying' in brackets.

a. Shakespeare is the greatest of all playwrights. (considered)

_____

_____

b. He travelled widely across Europe. (said)

_____

_____

c. Mrs Thatcher needs very little sleep. (said)

_____

_____

d. He was a member of the communist party when he was young. (known)

_____

_____

e. The rain will disappear this afternoon. (expected)

_____

_____

f. The escaped prisoner is heading for Scotland. (reported)

_____

_____

g. She has an income of over one hundred thousand pounds. (supposed)

_____

_____

h. Three people have been killed in an avalanche. (believed)

_____

_____

i. They were skiing in the area when the avalanche started. (presumed)

_____

_____

j. The super powers are heading for an agreement on nuclear weapons. (thought)

_____

_____

Review of tenses

5 Correcting mistakes

In the following sentences, there are some mistakes in tense usage. Find them and correct them.

a. I've phoned Justin at the office all morning, but I can't get hold of him. And we won't see him tonight, either. By the time we get home, he'll go out.

b. John expected to get a decent rise because he worked at the company for many years. He knew he sold more cars every year than any of his colleagues. He'd been selling cars all his life, and had known exactly what approach to adopt with every customer who came in.

c. **A** Did you see the Renoir exhibition?
   B No. Where's it on?
   A At the Academy. I've been twice. It's been wonderful. I never saw most of the pictures. They were quite new to me.
   B I'll try and get round to see it.
   A By the time you get round to it, it'll finish.

6 Producing the correct tenses

Put the verb in brackets in the correct tense.

Drama in the air at 2,000 ft

An Oxford amateur pilot (a) _____ (proclaim) a hero after his propeller flew off in mid-air.

The drama began at 2,000 feet as Hugh Smallwood (b) _____ (take) his six-year-old son for a half-term treat in his single-engined Fokker light aircraft. He told the Oxford Review how he brought his plane down safely in a field after going through every pilot's nightmare.

'My son Max (c) _____ (pester) me for ages to take him up. It was a nice day so we decided to go sight-seeing over Oxfordshire,' said Mr Smallwood. 'Everything (d) _____ (look) rosy as we (e) _____ (turn) for home, but then I noticed the propeller (f) _____ (disappear).

'I reassured Max that we (g) _____ (be) okay, and then did what any pilot (h) _____ (do) – we went into a glide and looked around for somewhere to land.

'I didn't have any time to make a mayday call, and spiralled down for the approach. Luckily the field was big enough.'

The cause of the mid-air mishap (i) _____ (remain) a mystery as Mr Smallwood (j) _____ (prepare) a report for the Air Accident Investigation Branch.

'For a moment I thought I (k) _____ (choose) the wrong place to land, but it turned out fine. I kept wondering 'What (I) _____ my wife (think)?'. Fire engines rushed to the scene, but both of them and the plane were unscathed.

Advertising director Mr Smallwood (m) _____ (own) the plane for seven years. The plane (n) _____ (date) from the 1950s, but Mr Smallwood said it (o) _____ (service) regularly and (p) _____ (fly) perfectly. The propeller (q) _____ (find) in the paddock of a nearby farm.

Irene Smallwood said, 'I don't think I (r) _____ (let) the children fly again.'

Brave Max said he wasn't frightened at the time. 'I knew my dad (s) _____ (get) us down.'

Air Accidents Officer Alan James said,'Hugh is obviously an accomplished pilot. I (t) _____ never (hear) of a propeller coming off like this, but he (u) _____ (cope) with it very well.

Said Mr Smallwood ' I (v) _____ (make) a forced landing before, but it's unusual to have two in a lifetime. In a way I (w) _____ (feel) quite privileged.'

And why (x) _____ he (y) _____ (take) up flying? 'For the excitement!'

7 Reacting to statistics

Study the following statistics about arms spending in the world, and then write a report outlining your reactions to them.

Comparative spending of 9 countries in 1984
Numbers = million US $

	Military	% of GNP*	Education	Health
France	23,106	4.1	29,507	37,149
Greece	3,049	7.2	1,006	1,543
Japan	12,364	1.0	63,550	56,874
Italy	10,652	2.7	22,217	23,107
Spain	4,492	2.4	4,600	8,528
United Kingdom	26,525	5.4	25,260	26,525
United States	237,052	6.4	182,520	159,500
USSR	225,400	11.5	91,800	62,700
W. Germany	21,956	3.3	30,953	54,482

* Gross National Product
(World Military and Social Expenditure 1987-88, Ruth Leger Sivard)

DEFENCE SPENDING

The estimated level of spending on armaments throughout the world is about $790,000 million £500,000 million. This represents £100 per person per annum, or 10 per cent of the world's total production of goods and services. In 1986 there were 27.2 million full-time armed force regulars or conscripts plus 42.6 million reservists and 30.8 million para-militaries to total more than 100 million.

The budgeted expenditure on defence by the US Government for the fiscal year 1986 was $273,369 million (£180 billion).

The defence burden on the USSR has been variously estimated as a percentage of GNP (gross national product) to be between 12 and 17 per cent and thus may nearly treble that of the US (6.4 per cent of GNP).

(*Guinness Book of Records*)

Some Indicators Of Our Madness

- To keep military expenses at their present levels, everyone during his lifetime will have to sacrifice from three to four years of his income to the arms race.

- The developed countries spend twenty times more on their military programs than on economic aid to the poor countries.

- In two days, the world spends on armaments what it costs the organization of the United Nations and its specialist agencies per year.

- More than 100 million citizens receive their wages directly or indirectly from Ministries of Defence.

- The training of military personnel in the United States costs twice as much each year as the budget for the education of 300 million children of school age in South Asia.

- The price of the Trident Submarine is equal to the cost of maintaining 16 million children in the developing countries in school for a year.

- For the price of one tank, 1,000 classrooms for 30,000 children could be built.

- For the price of one fighter plane, 40,000 village pharmacies could be set up.

Adapted from *World Military and Social Expenditures 1980*, by Ruth Leger Sivard. (c) World Priorities, Leesburg, Virginia 22075 and from *North-South : A Programme for Survival*, the Report of the Independent Commision on the Problems of International Development, MIT Press, Cambridge, Massachusetts, 1980.

8 Odd man out

In the following lists of words, three words rhyme. Circle the odd man out in each case.

a.	weird	beard	heard	cheered
b.	heir	prayer	fare	player
c.	sore	sew	awe	roar
d.	choose	loose	fuse	clues
e.	wool	dull	pull	bull
f.	fierce	spheres	peers	fears
g.	tough	rough	cough	enough
h.	lair	liar	buyer	wire
i.	iron	Ryan	lion	minion
j.	toad	loud	load	sewed
k.	danger	ranger	stranger	anger
l.	card	ward	hoard	sawed

9 'To break' and verbs with a similar meaning

Write one of the following verbs (in its correct form) in each space. Sometimes more than one verb is possible.

break	snap	splinter	crush
crack	burst	shatter	crumble

Literal meaning

a. A rubber band does this if you stretch it too much. _____

b. To make wine, you first _____ the grapes.

c. If a plate is this, you can still use it. _____

d. My children's toys don't last. They _____ very easily.

e. A vase would do this if you dropped it from a height. _____

f. Water pipes do this in cold weather. _____

g. You shouldn't give chicken bones to a dog because they _____ into small pieces.

h. This is what happens to cliffs over the years because of the action of the tide. _____

Metaphorical meaning

i. After a year fighting in the trenches, his nerve finally _____ and he had to be sent home.

j. The little boy _____ into tears when he couldn't find his mother.

k. His time of 9.06 seconds _____ the world record.

l. The injury _____ his dreams of becoming a professional footballer.

m. An army hopes to _____ its enemy.

n. If your temper does this, you suddenly get very angry! _____

o. A _____ group is a group of people who break away from a large organization to form their own group. (Use the verb as an adjective).

p. Empires grow and then _____ over the years, until nothing is left of them.

10 Idioms — their origins

The following extracts give both the origin and meaning of certain English idioms, but the actual idiom is omitted. Study them and try to work out what the idiom is. The correct answers are written upside down, beneath.

---

a. _____ is to forget old scores and let bygones be bygones, and comes from the American Indian custom of burying their hatchets, scalp-knives, and war clubs when making peace, to show that hostilities were at an end.

---

b. _____ is to receive the blame for a misdeed or mistake for which others are responsible. The phrase, which is still used widely in everyday life, was originally a military one, and referred to the person chosen to carry the beer cans to and fro for replenishingwhen they were empty. (A 'can' was a nickname for a simpleton, during World War I.)

---

c. _____ is to quarrel with someone very loudly. The analogy is to the work of the blacksmith who holds the hot iron with the tongs and brings the hammer down forcibly, and loudly, to beat the iron into shape. This also gives rise to other expressions such as 'hammering something home', or 'hammering an idea into someone's head'.

---

d. _____ is a warning that others might be listening when matters that are secret are being discussed. The phrase was used widely during World War II, along with others such as 'Careless talk costs lives', and 'Be like dad, keep mum!'

The warning is supposed to have been coined in the time of Catherine de Medici, who learnt of State secrets, and plots by listening through the walls of certain rooms.

---

e. _____ is to act on one's judgement, and be an independent person. Originally, the phrase came from the free companies of mercenary soldiers who roamed over Europe in the Middle Ages and were willing to sell their services to any cause or master. This meant, in effect, that they had not only offered themselves but their lances for hire.

Nowadays, the term 'freelance' refers to artists, journalists, writers, musicians and any other skilled people who are not on the salaried staff of any organization, but self-employed, who sell their talents on the free market to those willing to pay.

---

f. _____ is to take advantage of a situation, or act at the right time. This saying, which goes back to the 14th century, comes from the blacksmith who must strike the metal of a horseshoe when it is red hot, and at exactly the right temperature, to create the precise shape and fit required.

---

g. _____ is to be in charge and keep things going while others, normally responsible are absent. The phrase is best known for its use, in 1864, during the American Civil War, when General Sherman signalled to General Corse, from the top of Kennesaw, 'Hold the fort, at all costs'.

---

h. _____ someone, a group of people, or an organization, is to take the reins in one's own hands and go ahead with a course of action, without any consideration for the feelings or interests of others. The phrase comes from the days when it was common practice to ride rough-shod horses in which the nail-heads of the horseshoes were left projecting so that they could be ridden anywhere without slipping, particularly in icy conditions.

Answers

d. Walls have ears

c. To go at anyone, or anything, hammer and tongs

b. To carry the can

a. To bury the hatchet

h. To ride roughshod over

g. To hold the fort

f. To strike while the iron is hot

e. To be a freelance

11 Dependent prepositions

Write the correct preposition in each gap.

The CND

The Campaign (a) _____ Nuclear Disarmament (CND) is celebrating thirty years of

calling (b) _____ the removal (c) _____ Britain's nuclear weapons.

CND believes (d) _____ unilateral disarmament. The chairman of the organization,

Bruce Kent, says 'Ideas (e) _____

disarmament have changed (f) _____ the years. Russian and American leaders now agree that

an equal number of weapons (g) _____ both

sides is not necessary (h) _____ security, and

that major cuts (i) _____ nuclear arms should

be made. These ideas stemmed (j) _____

groups like CND, who have argued (k) _____ reductions for years.' CND was launched in London

in 1958 (l) _____ a meeting (m) _____

five thousand enthusiasts.

(n) _____ that time, Britain had just begun to

test its own H-bomb, and the policy (o) _____ having its own nuclear weapons to stop other

countries (p) _____ attacking had been made official.

By 1961, there were nearly one thousand CND

groups in Britain protesting (q) _____

increased expenditure (r) _____ nuclear arms. But since then, there has been a decline

(s) _____ membership. Bruce Kent explains,

'We failed (t) _____ our attempt to make

people see the connection (u) _____ declining social services and the fact that the government is

spending twelve billion pounds (v) _____ Trident missiles.'

UNIT 6

Adjective order

1 Matching adjectives with a noun

The jumbled words below can all be used as adjectives. Put them with an appropriate noun. Take care with the order of the adjectives that go with each noun.

thatched rich gripping

ivory

cocktail

plush

throbbing

chess

oriental

filling

constant

modernized

cosy

wide-mouthed

leafy

detective

bilingual

miserable

Victorian

booming

priceless

cold quiet

up-to-date mid-winter

loud posh beaming

a. a/an _____ dictionary

b. a/an _____ day

c. a/an _____ cottage

d. a/an _____ story

e. a/an _____ voice

f. a/an _____ meal

g. a/an _____ party

h. a/an _____ set

i. a/an _____ pain

j. a/an _____ grin

k. a/an _____ suburb

l. a/an _____ carpet

2 Describing clothes

Look at the pictures of clothes on pages 62 and 63 of the Student's Book. Write phrases describing some of them. The chart below will help you with the order of the adjectives.

Value	Detail	Material	Noun
smart	blue	cotton	trousers
scruffy	old	denim	shirt

_____

_____

_____

_____

_____

Adverbs

3 Adverbs with two forms

Underline the correct form of the adverb.

A Can I help myself to a coffee?
B Feel (a) **free/freely**!
A Can I speak to you (b) **free/freely** and (c) **direct/directly**?
B Of course.
A Will you give me your honest reaction?
B That's (d) **easier/more easily** said than done. I'm (e) **most/mostly** honest, but not all the time, I (f) **free/freely** admit. Have I done something (g) **wrong/wrongly**?
A Come (h) **close/closely** to me and see what I've found.

(Her eyes opened (i) **wide/widely** as she saw the object in his hand. She examined it (j) **close/closely**, and then began to laugh out (k) **loud/loudly**.)

A I am (l) **most/mostly** upset that you should react in this way. Remember, I have a (m) **high/highly** respected position. I found this substance, which I suspect to be a drug of some kind, (n) **right/rightly** in the middle of your cereal bowl.
B You (o) **right/rightly** assume that it is a drug, but you (p) **wrong/wrongly** suspect that I have it illegally. It is my prescription. You (q) **hard/hardly** notice me any more. I have been taking it (r) **late/lately** because I have been suffering from migraine. I am now leaving you. I am flying (s) **direct/directly** to Moscow.
A My word! You travel (t) **light/lightly**! Are you only taking a briefcase?

4 Adverbs and expressions of opinion – definition

Match the adverbs and expressions of opinion with the definitions of their functions underneath each paragraph.

I know you don't like Susan, but (a) **quite honestly**, I think I'm old enough to look after myself now. (b) **After all**, I'm nearly thirty, and a lot of my friends have been married for ages. (c) **By the way**, did you hear that Glynn and his wife have had twins? No, not a boy and a girl, two girls, (d) **actually**. I wish you'd realize what a lovely girl Susan is. (e) **Anyway**, I love her, and that's all there is to it.

1 _____ I am changing the subject to introduce something new.

2 _____ What I said before doesn't matter. This is the main point.

3 _____ I am trying to persuade you by presenting an argument that you haven't properly considered.

4 _____ This is my honest opinion.

5 _____ I am correcting you by pointing out a fact that you weren't aware of.

(f) **Naturally**, I understand that you want to be independent, and (g) **obviously**, you and Susan have a lot in common, but (h) **surely** you appreciate my concern? (i) **Admittedly**, she is a very pleasant girl, and she has a good job so (j) **presumably** she's intelligent, but I do wonder if she's the girl for you. (k) **Basically**, I think you're rushing into this relationship too quickly, and (l) **personally** I think you are still too young. (m) **Ideally**, a man should be thirty-five before he begins to look for a wife. You've only known her for three months! (n) **Generally speaking**, the longer a couple know each other before committing the rest of their lives to each other, the more chance there is of the union lasting. And I've heard some not very pleasant things about Susan. I was talking to Mrs Brewin the other day, and (o) **apparently**, Susan was engaged to be married only last year, and then called it off at the last minute! So, be warned, my boy! (p) **Strictly speaking**, as your guardian, I can still forbid this marriage, but I would rather persuade you myself of the wisdom of my words.

6 _____ This would be the perfect situation.

7 _____ This is my basic point.

8 _____ This is not surprising, it is to be expected.

9 _____ This cannot be doubted, everyone knows about it.

10 _____ This is something I've heard, but I'm not sure of.

11 _____ This is so obvious that I would be surprised if you disagreed with me.

12 _____ This is my personal opinion.

13 _____ This is an opinion that is true in most situations.

14 _____ This is something I suppose is true, but I'm not certain.

15 _____ This is a point which goes against what I am saying and weakens my argument.

16 _____ I am giving you precise information about a situation.

5 Adverbs and expressions of opinion – practice

Underline the most appropriate adverb or expression of opinion.

January 14

Dear Joey

Thanks for your letter telling us what time your plane arrives.

(a) **Presumably/Frankly/Obviously/Naturally**, we'll be at the airport to meet you. Don't worry about me having to take a day off work.

(b) **As a matter of fact/After all/Surely/Basically**, it's not every day that your only daughter comes home from the States! You didn't say where you would be staying while you're here (c) **Presumably/Admittedly/Incidentally/Anyway**, you'll be at home with us for a few days and then head off to visit your friends.

We were sorry to hear that you have left your job. (d) **Naturally/Generally speaking/Ideally/Admittedly**, being a waitress is not the most glamorous job in the world, but (e) **at least/strictly speaking/obviously/honestly** it pays the bills. (f) **Naturally/Actually/Surely/After all** you're being a little ambitious trying to be a pop singer!

In your last letter you said you were thinking of going to college to finish your education, and (g) **anyway/after all/apparently/basically** I think this is the best thing you could do. I was talking to some colleagues who have studied in the States. (h) **Presumably/Apparently/Actually/Incidentally**, students can get grants on a loan basis, which sounds fine for you. Do think about this.

(i) **By the way/As a matter of fact/Anyway/Ideally**, I must finish now. The weather is freezing here. Mum sends her love. (j) **Obviously/Apparently/Basically/Honestly** we're all very excited about seeing you again.

See you very soon.

Love

Dad

---

6 Order of adverbs

Put the adverbial phrases in brackets in an appropriate place in the sentence.

a. I read that there have been several near misses. (in the skies; recently; the other day; over London; in the paper)

b. I have liked travelling by air. (really; personally; never)

c. I fly if it is essential, but I try to get out of it. (always; only; then; absolutely; even)

d. I can't understand how something weighing two hundred tons can fly. (just; easily; frankly; so)

e. I can understand how some people like flying. (very much; quite; however)

f. I was talking to a boy who wants to be a pilot. (only; in fact; yesterday)

g. He wants to go hang-gliding. (also; actually)

h. He has thought about going, but he has done it. (never; often; actually)

i. He said he felt nervous at take-off and landing. (slightly; sometimes; even)

j. I am getting used to flying, but I don't think I will enjoy it. (ever; slowly; fortunately; still; actually)

Writing

7 Describing a scene

Describe the scenes in the picture from the viewpoint of TWO of the following people.

A ten-year-old girl
A policeman
A blind person
A visitor from another country

Pronunciation

8 Linking vowel to vowel

Practise saying the following words.

the apple /ðɪjæpl/
free entrance /fri:jentrəns/
my uncle /maijʌŋkl/
pay up /peɪjʌp/

When the sounds /ɪ/, /i:/, /eɪ/, and /aɪ/ come at the end of a word and the next word begins with a vowel sound, there is often an extra /j/ to link them.

Practise saying the following words.

blue eyes /blu:waɪz/
no understanding /nəʊwʌndəstændɪŋ/
how easy /haʊwi:zɪ/

When the sounds /u:/, /əʊ/, and /aʊ/ come at the end of a word and the next word begins with a vowel sound, there is often an extra /w/ to link them.

Remember that /r/ is also sounded at the end of a word if the next word begins with a vowel sound.

Peter is coming /pi:tərɪzkʌmɪŋ/

Practice 1

In the following sentences, mark where the links are and put in the linking /j/, /w/, and /r/ sounds.

a. The awful aunty is here in a new outfit.
b. The doctor advised me to eat only apples.
c. The author is an ugly individual who earns a lot.
d. A new Austin is too expensive for us to afford.
e. I've got three oranges for me and you.
f. He and Hugh Appleby are thirty-eight years old.

Practice 2

Here is part of Tapescript 14 from page 151 of the Student's Book. Mark where the links are, put in the extra linking sounds, and then mark where you think the main sentence stresses are. Listen to the tape again to check your answers. The first sentence has been done for you.

Quite honestly, I don't know how you've put up

with it for all these years. Personally, I would have

left after a few weeks. After all, it's not as though it

was your fault. I mean to say, he was the one that

was so keen on it in the first place. Actually, he had

to work really hard to persuade you, if I remember

rightly. Frankly, I think you should remind him of that

a bit more often. You are still speaking to each other,

presumably? I wouldn't blame you if you weren't!

Seriously though, enough is enough! Admittedly, he

wasn't to know, but he should have made it his job to

find out! After all, he always prides himself on his

thoroughness!

Vocabulary

9 Colours

Match a word in box **A** with a colour in box **B** to make a shade of a colour.

A		B
blood	emerald	blue
pitch	brick	brown
nut	slate	green
jet	apple	grey
salmon	snow	red
shocking	navy	pink
bottle	sky	white
cherry	olive	black

10 Gap filling – 'The Windsor jewels'

Write one suitable word in each gap.

The Windsor jewels

Wallis collection dazzles bidders

By Dalya Alberge

Geneva gems: A ruby and diamond necklace, and flamingo clip.

The collection of (a) _____ jewels being sold by Sotheby's for 'over £10m' is (b) _____ for a queen. For their owner, the Duchess of Windsor, however, they could only ever be a substitute for the crown. Although she demanded that her servants (c) _____ her as 'Your Royal Highness', she became instead a larger-than-life queen of 1940s fashion and style.

It was in 1936 that King Edward VIII sensationally (d) _____ from the throne to marry Wallis Simpson, an American divorcee. They left for Paris in 1937.

The Duke was a man with a (e) _____ eye for gems and style; he (f) _____ Wallis with ostentatious gifts that celebrated events in their life together.

It is sad to reflect that the Duke (g) _____ in his will that his wife's jewels should never adorn another woman. He would have been horrified to learn that more than 3,000 people had booked a place for the sale.

'Thousands have been (h) _____ the items each day, both in New York and Geneva,' one overwhelmed Sotheby's representative reported. Among the rich and fashionable who are believed to have been dazzled into (i) _____ are the queen of television soap, Joan Collins, and the pop musician, Elton John.

This seems to be the closing (j) _____ in the romance, and like all good stories, it combines history, money and love. Many of the 200 jewels are unique mementoes with personal and now historic inscriptions (k) _____ particular events.

'Historical events can be followed through inscriptions on a remarkable number of pieces,' the sale catalogue says. 'In this respect, the Duke was himself following a family (l) _____.'

One hundred years earlier, Prince Albert had dates and messages (m) _____ on some of the jewellery that he gave to Queen Victoria.

Sotheby's experts believe the three elements of history, quality and design make the collection altogether (n) _____. There is, for example, the Duchess's favourite Van Cleef and Arpels necklace with intertwined rows of rubies and diamonds. It was commissioned by the Duke of Windsor as her 40th birthday present, and is engraved: 'My Wallis from her David 19/6/36' – the year of the abdication (estimate £500,000 – £620,000).

The (o) _____ of the sale will be donated towards medical research. The beneficiary is the Pasteur Institute in Paris.

11 Crossword puzzle

Here is another crossword puzzle for you to try!

ACROSS

1 Pink flowers with frilly petals, often worn as buttonholes (10)
8 Not in favour of (7)
9 One of the signs of the zodiac (5)
10 A short letter (4)
11 You see one in the sky or on the screen! (4)
12 To make a mistake (3)
14 The opposite of a vice (6)
15 Another word for empty — you hope a hotel has a _____ room (6)
18 Another word for to decay. This is what food does if you leave it for a long time (3)
20 To control or restrain (4)
21 Another word for naked — we talk about the _____ facts (4)
23 Belonging to a town — we talk about _____ development (5)
24 A dried grape, used especially in cakes (7)
25 A formal word for improvement (10)

DOWN

1 Section of a book (7)
2 What a tenant pays (4)
3 Another word for perceptive — we talk about an _____ comment (6)

4 Another word for to abuse, for example, an animal (3-5)
5 Honest, deserving respect — we talk about a _____ action (5)
6 Meat-eating (11)
7 An idiom meaning to take the blame — you had it in Unit 5 of this book! (5,3,3)
13 Concise, clear, to the point and in few words — we talk about a _____ account (8)
16 Determined not to change your mind (7)
17 You use this to rub things out (6)
19 A common item of furniture (5)
22 A kind of adhesive (4)

Multi-word verbs

12 Multi-word verbs — type 4

In many type 4 multi-word verbs (which consist of a verb + adverb + preposition), the adverb is used quite literally, and serves to intensify or enrich the verb meaning.

Keep away from *me! I've got a cold.*
She **walked out on** *her family and left them to fend for themselves.*
You know that job we saw in the paper! I've **written off for** *an application form.*

Matching

How many combinations of verb from column **A** and adverb and preposition from column **B** do you know?

A	B
cut	up for
come	up to
do	down on
face	behind with
make	up with
speak	in for
go	up against
fall	away with
fit	through with
keep	in with
own	along with

Gap filling

Fill each gap with one of the adverb + preposition combinations. **Up for**, **up to**, and **up with** are used twice.

a. Once you begin to fall _____ _____ your monthly repayments, it's very difficult to catch up.

b. Stop letting people walk all over you! You should speak _____ _____ what you believe in.

c. Her husband died when they were both sixty-five, and although she had many interests of her own, nothing could make _____ _____ the loss of her life-long companion.

d. The government has come _____ _____ a lot of criticism over its handling of the economy.

e. We'll have to cut _____ _____ the amount we spend on food. It's costing us a fortune!

f. The arrival of computers has done _____ _____ a lot of boring paper work.

g. 'To keep _____ _____ the Joneses' is an expression that means to try to have all the possessions that your neighbours have because you don't want to seem inferior.

h. It is very common for people to feel nervous on their wedding day. They think they can't possibly go _____ _____ it, but then they are swept up by the events of the day, and their doubts disappear.

i. Police have come _____ _____ a new problem in their fight against crime. They are finding that criminals have access to police computers, and they are changing the data on their own files.

j. Now I'm forty I'll just have to face _____ _____ the fact that I'm not as young as I was!

k. The new furniture fits _____ well _____ the rest of the room. The colours really blend together.

l. The company was facing ruin, but someone came _____ _____ an idea for a new product which really swept the market.

m. I've lost my favourite pen. No-one has owned _____ _____ taking it, so I'll just have to buy a new one.

n. I don't go _____ _____ all her political views, but I think she's got the right ideas about education.

UNIT 7

Verb patterns

1 Using the information in a learner's dictionary

Some of the verb patterns in the following sentences are right, and some are wrong. Look at the dictionary extracts to decide which are which, and correct those that are wrong.

> **agree** /əˈgriː/ v 1 [I, Ipr, It] ~ (to sth) say 'yes'; say that one is willing; consent (to sth): *I asked for a pay rise and she agreed.* ○ *Is he going to agree to our suggestion?* ○ *He agreed to let me go home early.* Cf REFUSE². 2 (a) [I, Ipr, It, Tf, Tw] ~ (with sb) (about/on sth); ~ (with sb) (about sb); ~ (with sth) be in harmony (with sb); have or form a similar opinion (as sb): *When he said that, I had to agree.* ○ *Do you agree with me about the need for more schools?* ○ *We couldn't agree on a date/agree when to meet.* ○ *I agree with his analysis of the situation.* ○ *We agreed to start early.* ○ *Do we all agree that the proposal is a good one?* Cf DISAGREE.

a. He thinks we should go and I am agree.
b. She agreed on me that we should have a party.
c. She agreed that we should go home.
d. She thought we should go, and I agreed it.
e. They agreed on fighting the proposal was a bad idea.
f. Pat and Peter agree with most things.
g. We don't agree about politics, so we'll have to agree to differ.

> **ad·vise** /ədˈvaɪz/ v 1 [Ipr, Tn, Tn·pr, Tf, Tw, Tg, Dn·f, Dn·w, Dn·t] ~ (sb) against sth/doing sth; ~ sb (on sth) give advice to sb; recommend: *The doctor advised (me to take) a complete rest.* ○ *They advised her against marrying quickly.* ○ *She advises the Government on economic affairs.* ○ *We advised that they should start early/advised them to start early.* ○ *I'd advise taking a different approach.* ○ *You would be well advised* (ie sensible) *to stay indoors.* ○ *Can you advise (me) what to do next?*

h. He advised to try again next year.
i. She advised me against buying government bonds.
j. He advised them a service their new car every six months.
k. My accountant advises me for all financial matters.

> **force²** /fɔːs/ v 1 [Tn·pr, Cn·t] make (sb/oneself) do sth he/one does not want to do; compel; oblige: *force a confession out of sb* ○ *The thief forced her to hand over the money.* ○ *He forced himself to speak to her.* ○ *The president was forced into resigning/to resign.*

l. She forced herself eating even though she wasn't hungry.
m. She tried to resist for years, but eventually she was forced into having an operation.
n. She forced to get a pay rise by threatening to resign.

> **per·suade** /pəˈsweɪd/ v 1 [Tn, Tn·pr, Cn·t] ~ sb (into/out of sth) cause sb to do sth by arguing or reasoning with him: *You try and persuade her (to come out with us).* ○ *He is easily persuaded.* ○ *How can we persuade him into joining us?* ○ *He persuaded his daughter to change her mind.* 2 [Tn esp passive, Tn·pr esp passive, Dn·f] ~ sb (of sth) (*fml*) cause sb to believe sth; convince sb: *I am not fully persuaded by the evidence.* ○ *We are persuaded of the justice of her case.* ○ *How can I persuade you that I am sincere?*

o. She persuaded to me to let her go.
p. I was persuaded not doing it.
q. He persuaded me into lending him a fortune.
r. She persuaded that her idea was best.

2 Verb patterns in reported speech

Report the following direct speech, using the verbs given.

'Why don't you accept the offer?' I said to her.

a. I suggested _____

b. I advised _____

c. I recommended _____

'You really must settle your debts,' he said to me.

d. He insisted _____

44

e. He told _____

f. He ordered _____

g. He made _____

h. He urged _____

'I'll pay you back tomorrow,' she said to me.

i. She said _____

j. She told _____

k. She explained _____

l. She promised _____

m. She insisted _____

'Please, please let me come with you,' she said to her father.

n. She begged _____

o. She pleaded _____

Conditional sentences

3 Conditional tenses and verb forms

Put the verb in brackets in an appropriate tense or verb form. Where there is no verb, - - -, insert an auxiliary verb. Sometimes more than one form is possible.

I met my wife while I was on a cruise. I fell ill, and she was the ship's doctor. Now we run a health food

shop. Just think! If I (a) _____

(not go) on that cruise and (b) _____

_____ (fall) ill, I (c) _____ (not

marry) her, our children (d) _____

(not be born) and I (e) _____

still _____ (work) as a teacher.

I haven't got a car, but if I (f) __ __ __, I (g)

_____ (be able) to drive into the

country at the weekend. I think I (h) _____

_____ (try) to buy one as soon as I

(i) _____ (can). It (j)

_____ (be) so convenient.

Harry is a remarkable chap! He's sixty now, and

(k) _____ (work) all his life

as a designer. He (l) _____
(retire) next year. He has so much talent that he

(m) _____ (make) a success of

any job he (n) _____ (turn) his
hand to, but he always says he is happy in what he

(o) _____ (do). I think he

(p) _____ (be) a very good
administrator in something like the Civil Service. He

(q) _____ (can) (rise) very high
in it, maybe even to ministerial level. On the other

hand, I don't think he (r) _____
(enjoy) it so much as being a designer, where he

(s) _____ (be) his own boss.

4 Mixed conditionals

Write conditional sentences combining types 2 and 3 for the following situations (see the Student's Book, page 140). The first two have been started for you.

a. Anne and John are having a row because she borrowed his tennis racket and lost it.

   They wouldn't _____

   _____

b. Jane is a very reliable journalist. That is why she was promoted to desk editor.

   If she weren't _____

   _____

c. I'm afraid of travelling by air, so I had to go to America by boat.

   _____

   _____

d. Justin's broke because he spent all his money on a music centre.

   _____

   _____

e. She doesn't know anything about first aid, so she couldn't help him.

   _____

   _____

45

f. I didn't look after my teeth, and now I've got false ones.

_____

_____

g. There's a good programme on television tonight, but I've already said to Ben that I'd see him in the pub.

_____

_____

h. What a pity I couldn't watch that programme last night! What a pity I haven't got a video recorder.

_____

_____

i. You're so gullible! How could you believe the lies he told you?

_____

_____

j. I'm going out to the theatre tonight, so I couldn't accept Peter's invitation to go round for a meal.

_____

_____

5 Variations on Types 1 and 2

Rewrite the following sentences using either **should** or **happen to** for type 1 conditionals or **were to** for type 2 conditionals, to express remote possibility. Remember that 'should' is quite formal; 'happen to' is less formal.

a. If you come across Henry, tell him to get in touch.
b. If you have any cause for complaint, please return the goods immediately.
c. If the negotiations broke down, the consequences for the whole country would be disastrous.
d. If you find my scarf, could you tell me?
e. If he ever found out what I'd done with his money, he'd never forgive me.
f. If guests wish to have breakfast in their own room, they are requested to inform Reception before retiring.
g. If we found life on another planet, I wonder how we would communicate?
h. If I see some shoes you'd like at the shops, I'll buy them for you.

6 Possible results

Complete the following sentences in an appropriate way, using either **might** or **could** + an infinitive (present or past).

a. If I don't have too much work tonight, I

_____

_____.

b. My car's being repaired at the moment. Sorry. If I had it, I

_____

_____.

c. If I earned more money, I

_____

_____.

d. Four people died in a fire at their home. If they had had a smoke detector, they

_____

_____.

e. If you were more understanding of other people,

_____

_____.

f. If it's a nice day on Sunday, we

_____

_____.

g. I've got terrible toothache. If the dentist decides I've got a bad tooth,

_____

_____.

h. The ship had no life boats, and twenty-five people drowned. If

_____

_____.

i. I started writing poetry after I'd met a famous poet at a cocktail party. He encouraged me to start. If

_____

_____.

j. It's a lovely day, and the sea's beautifully warm. What a pity we didn't bring our swimming costumes! If

_____

_____.

7 Writing a report

There was an armed raid on a security van outside Barclays Bank, Newtown, today. You are a reporter, and interviewed three witnesses. From their accounts write a report of the crime, giving the facts and quoting the witnesses where relevant.

PC Chris Green

'At about 11.17 am we heard on our car radio that a security van had been hijacked as it was being unloaded at Barclays Bank in Albion Road. We immediately rushed to the scene, just in time to see the security guards being locked into their own van by two men in grey balaclavas. They leapt into a white Ford Escort, dropping at least two bags. There must have been a third man behind the wheel, and they drove off at great speed. Of course, we gave chase, but the guy in the back started shooting at us. We were unarmed and couldn't return the shots. One shot narrowly missed PC Dixon, the radio operator, and as they turned a corner, another shot penetrated the driver's door and hit me in the right leg. I only just managed to stop the car and pull over to the kerb. I was bleeding profusely and in great pain. I don't remember anything after that — I must have blacked out.'

Liz Leigh, a secretary

'I was just coming out of the bank, and putting my money into my purse when I heard this almighty crash. It must have been just after 11.00 because I'd slipped out of the office in my coffee break. I looked up and saw this white car crashing into the front of the security van. Three men got out. Two of them were in balaclavas, but they were young. One was wearing jeans and was thin, and the other had a black leather jacket and was wearing trainers. He was a bit plumper. I didn't get a good look at the third one because I backed into the doorway of the bank. They yelled, 'Get out! get out!' at the driver of the van, and he obviously didn't move fast enough because they wrenched open the door and dragged him out and held a gun at his head while he opened the back of the van. Then they went wild, shoving him and his partner in the back while they grabbed at the bags of money. There were bags of money all over the street. Then they heard the police siren and started screaming at each other, 'Get a move on!' and dropping even more money about the place. I was terrified they'd notice me and point the gun at me. When the police arrived, they drove off. I think I heard some shots from down the street. I was stunned, but I got the number of the car. It was B180 VHS.'

Kevin Billings, a hospital porter

'I didn't know what was happening. I thought they were making a film at first. I came round the corner, and this fellow barged into me and knocked me over. He had a shotgun, and he fired it into the air and at the same time shouted, 'Keep down or I'll shoot you!' He was in his forties, greying, and he had a Scottish accent. That's when I realized it wasn't a film. I really thought I was going to die. He kept his foot on top of me while his mates rushed past into a car. I had my head down on the pavement. I couldn't see anything, and I kept expecting a final shot in the head. I heard sirens and there was a banging of doors and the screech of tyres and they were gone. I heard shots then, but down the road. Two, I think. I feel really lucky to be alive.'

Pronunciation

8 How do you pronounce '-ough'?

Put the following words into the correct column, according to the pronunciation of -ough.

cough though through ought fought thorough dough
tough trough enough sought drought thought
bough nought plough rough bought borough

/ɔ:/ (6 words)	/ʌf/ (3 words)	/ɒf/ (2 words)	/u:/ (1 word)	/ə/ (2 words)	/əʊ/ (2 words)	/aʊ/ (3 words)

Here are fourteen further words that rhyme with the different pronunciations of **-ough**.
Put them in the correct boxes in the columns below. There are two per column.

caught   *toff*ee   ter*ror*   cuff   groan   doubt   burg*lar*
snuff   frown   glow   warn   off   stew   queue

/ɔː/	/ʌf/	/ɒf/	/uː/	/ə/	/əʊ/	/aʊ/

Vocabulary

9 Replacing 'nice' and 'get'

In the following story, **nice** and **get** are overused.
Replace them with a more precise word or phrase
where possible. (Sometimes, **get** is almost impossible
to replace.) Let your imagination wander a little to
see if you can find other ways of expressing the same
idea.

Brian Brownlee | got a good night's sleep, *slept soundly, slept like a log,* | and got up

(can't change) | nice and early, *at the crack of dawn* | got dressed in *put on*

his | nicest *best* clothes and had a *smartest* | nice *full* breakfast. *light nourishing*

He turned on the radio to get the news headlines,
which weren't nice. 'Three people got killed in a car
crash last night, and Bill Todd got re-elected as
president of the Miners' Union.' He turned the radio
off. 'The news really gets me down,' he said to his
wife. He gave her a nice kiss and set off for work.
Outside it was a nice day. Brian got into his car but
he couldn't get it going. 'I'll have to get this car
fixed,' he thought. 'It really gets me when it won't
start straight away.'

He got to work at 9.00, and went to his office, which
was very nice with lots of nice furniture. It had a
nice view over the park. He got out his diary and
phoned his secretary.

'Get me Mr Atkins on the phone, please.' Mr Atkins
was a nice old customer, but he always haggled about
prices.

'I must get him to accept my terms,' Brian thought.

'Hello, Brian,' said Mr Atkins. 'I hear you've been
promoted. That's nice news!'

'How did you get to hear that?' replied Brian.

'A little birdie told me.'

'I don't get it.'

'Never mind. Now listen. Your price sounds nice, but
I'd like to bring the delivery date forward.'

'Now we're getting somewhere. When to?'

'Three weeks' time would be nice for us.'

'Fine. Bye-bye. Have a nice day!'

10 Compound words

Make compound words according to the definitions,
using the word in bold as the first word of the
compound.

Use your dictionary to see if the compound is written
as one word or with a hyphen, and mark the stress.
Sometimes the stress is on the first word, and
sometimes the second.

by

a. _____ Something that is made in the manufacture of something else.

b. _____ The voting for a member of Parliament to replace a previous member who has resigned or died.

over

c. _____ To repair, clean and check thoroughly a machine or other piece of equipment.

d. _____ The sky is this when there are a lot of clouds and the light is bad.

e. _____ These are the regular and essential expenses of a business, for example, the rent, the phone, electricity.

f. _____ These are what mechanics wear to protect their clothes.

g. _____ If someone falls off a ship, they are this.

h. _____ A careless mistake made because one has failed to notice something important.

i. _____ To behave in an exaggerated way, or to work too hard.

j. _____ If you take this, you take more of a drug than is safe.

under

k. _____ The person who has learned an actor's part and can replace him/her in case of illness.

l. _____ Bushes and plants growing together under the trees in a forest or jungle.

m. _____ To not realize how large or important something is.

n. _____ Part of an aeroplane, including the wheels, which supports it when it is on the ground, taking off and landing.

o. _____ This kind of agent is operating secretly to obtain information for the police or a government.

p. _____ If an organization is this, it doesn't have enough employees to operate properly.

q. _____ Inadequately or badly fed.

r. _____ Person whose job it is to look after the bodies of people who have died and to arrange their funerals.

11 Idioms — key words

Read the following dialogue and choose the correct key word to complete the idioms.

Use your dictionary to check your answers.

Two robbers, Harry the Grab and Mini Murphy, have just escaped from the police and are hiding in a warehouse.

Harry: That was a near thing. We got away just (a) **in the** | edge / nick | **of time**. Get down behind those boxes and we'll (b) **sit** | tight / close | until Max and the rest of the gang arrive.

Mini: How do they know where to find us? We could be here for a (c) **month of** | Sundays / holidays | and we've got nothing to eat. I'll look around and see how the (d) | place / land | **lies**. What's that noise?

Harry: Shut up and keep still or you'll (e) **give the** | match / game | **away**. It's the night-watchman. He must have (f) **smelled a** | rat / rabbit |. His torch is getting nearer — Oh no — look — the police!

Policeman: Hello! Hello! Hello! If it isn't Harry the Grab and Mini Murphy. (g) **The** | match / game | **is up**, Mad Max has (h) **spilt the** | beans / salt | **on you** lot. He's told us everything so you may as well (i) **throw in the** | glove / towel |.

Harry: What do you mean officer? You're (j) **barking up the wrong** | tree / avenue |, we've been drinking in the King's Head all evening.

Policeman: It's no good Harry. We've got all the evidence we need. You (k) **haven't got a** | foot / leg | **to stand on.** You'll be (l) **doing** | time / days | again before long. No one will be able to (m) **get you off the** | nail / hook | this time, not even the best lawyer in the land!

Now complete the idiom and check the meaning.

in the _____ of time	— only just in time
to sit _____	— to stay firmly in one place
a month of _____	— a very long time
to see how the _____ lies	— to find out the exact situation
to give the _____ away	— to betray a secret, with or without intention
to smell a _____	— to suspect that something is wrong
the _____ is up	— the plan is discovered
to spill the _____	— to say something that people have been trying to keep secret
to throw in the _____	— to admit defeat
to bark up the wrong _____	— to direct an inquiry or accusation at the wrong place or person
to not have a _____ to stand on	— to have nothing to support your argument
to do _____	— to be in prison
to get sb off the _____	— to solve a difficult situation for sb

12 Dependent prepositions

Write the correct preposition in each gap.

Television and reading

I pride myself (a) _____ the fact that I read two or three books a week. (b) _____ this rate I'll be familiar (c) _____ every book in our local library soon.

I blame TV (d) _____ the way people don't seem to read as much as they used to. (e) _____ my way of thinking TV is responsible (f) _____ many ills in our society.

I wonder (g) _____ the amount of TV watched by my sister's children. I have warned her (h) _____ the dangers of this but (i) _____ vain. She refuses to get involved (j) _____ a discussion (k) _____ the subject.

(l) _____ one time I used to watch a fair amount of TV but I restricted myself (m) _____ particular programmes such as documentaries and an occasional good film. However I soon grew tired (n) _____ even this. I was indifferent (o) _____ many of the topics in the documentaries and there is always something missing (p) _____ films or TV plays which are based (q) _____ the stories in books. However good the film, it is no substitute (r) _____ the original story. At last I think I am beginning to convince my sister (s) _____ the bad effect of TV (t) _____ her children. She has agreed (u) _____ my suggestion of selective viewing and at the beginning of each week her family agrees (v) _____ which programmes they want to watch and the TV is only turned on at those times. It's taken a long time to get her to agree (w) _____ me but I'm sure the schoolwork of my nephews and niece will benefit as a result.

UNIT 8

1 Narrative tenses

Read the following short paragraph, and work out the order in which the guests arrived at the party.

By the time I got to Paula and Bob's party, Rob had left ages ago. Pat and Peter were late, as usual. Barbara and Tim had just arrived, and Simon, who'd been there for ages, was serving them with some things to nibble. Tony was already a bit tipsy, and was picking quarrels with anyone who'd listen. Apparently that's why Rob had left. He'd hardly taken his coat off when Tony started going on at him, so he just upped and left. When Angela had seen Tony arriving, she told Simon to keep an eye on how much he had to drink. Angela had got there early to help Paula, and was busy in the kitchen. When I asked Jim and Chris what Tony had said to Rob, they couldn't tell me because they hadn't heard anything. They didn't even know that Rob had been there. They'd arrived soon after Simon, and had been stuck in conversation with Bob ever since. I opened the door to let in Alice, so she and I settled down for a good chat and a gossip about Pat and Peter before they arrived. All in all, it was quite a good party.

Rob _____

Pat and Peter _____

Barbara and Tim _____

Me _____

Simon _____

Tony _____

Angela _____

Jim and Chris _____

Alice _____

2 Tense review (1)

Put the verbs in brackets in an appropriate tense.

A man whose cat (a) _____ (bite) by a dog (b) _____ (look) for a box in which to take the cat to the vet. The only box he could find was one which (c) _____ (use) to store a frozen turkey. At the surgery, the vet (d) _____ (peer) closely at the large label on the box: 'DEEP FROZEN TURKEY'.

'To be honest,' he remarked, shaking his head, 'I don't think there's much I can do about this.'

A man who (e) _____ (know) for his mean habits (f) _____ (go) shopping with his wife. As his birthday (g) _____ (come) soon, she (h) _____ (try) to buy him a card. She (i) _____ just _____ (select) one when her husband (j) _____ (take) the card from her hands and (k) _____ (read) the inscription inside. 'Thank you, dear,' he said, putting the card back on the shelves.

An interesting thing happened when I was touring the United States recently. I (l) _____ just _____ (read) a spy novel, where the hero (m) _____ (hide) a letter in a particular statue in Washington. Since I was in that city at the time, on a whim I decided to see if the statue really contained the small niche the author (n) _____ (describe). To my great surprise it did — and a letter was inside. After a moment's hesitation, I pulled out the letter and opened it. When I (o) _____ (read) it, I burst out laughing. An unidentified reader (p) _____ (write): 'Good book, wasn't it?'

JUNK STORY THAT BEAT THE EXPERTS

The strangest story I (a) _____ever _____ (report) began one Spring morning in Hong Kong. I was born and brought up in Hong Kong and I (b) _____just _____ (start) working as a radio reporter there.

In March 1981, ninety-five fishing junks (c) _____(spot) sailing over the horizon. Immediately they (d) _____(surround) by police launches who thought they were trying (e) _____(sneak) into Hong Kong against the law.

One of Hong Kong's greatest problems is trying to keep out thousands of people who think life there (f) _____(be) better than in China, and try to smuggle themselves in. Hong Kong is already the most crowded place in the world, and there's no room for more people.

But when the police asked the junk people why they (g) _____(come) they (h) _____(get) a shock. They said they (i) _____(stay) for a few days (j) _____(escape) the terrible calamity that was about (k) _____(strike) their villages in China.

They said there was complete panic at home because everyone (l) _____(believe) an earthquake (m) _____(come).

Throughout its history China (n) _____(suffer) terrible earthquakes, cities (o) _____(destroy) and thousands killed. Nowadays, all over the country there are seismographic centres where earthquakes can easily (p) _____(predict).

The Hong Kong authorities phoned one of these centres in China to find out whether they (q) _____(warn) about a forthcoming earthquake, but the answer was no. Experts in Hong Kong agreed that there was no reason for the junk people's fears.

Consequently the junk people (r) _____(send) home. On their way back an earthquake did indeed (s) _____(strike) their village. No-one was hurt but the mystery (t) _____(remain). How did the junk people know, when the scientists and experts with all their sophisticated machines didn't?

4 Punctuation

Punctuate the following sentences in an appropriate way.

a. my childrens cries of excitement woke me up with a start look daddy they shouted weve found a birds nest its got eggs in it too thats lovely i said but come away from it or the bird will be too worried about its nest

b. i packed everything i needed for the journey in a small leather hold all books a change of clothes some sandwiches and some of my mothers home made cake

c. the queen who led the country during the period of its greatest industrial supremacy was queen victoria

d. the queen who spends much of her time travelling is well loved by her people

e. mr higginss butchers shop is the best in the area

f. theres no point in reading that newspaper she said its out of date

g. the bbc starts transmitting programmes at six am

h. could you get a pounds worth of three inch nails from the ironmongers

5 Writing a story

1 Read the following outline of a story by Oscar Wilde.

The Selfish Giant

There was a giant who lived in a castle surrounded by a large garden. The giant went away to visit his friend the Cornish Ogre. He was away for seven years.

During that time children from the village came to play in the garden.

When the giant returned he was furious to see the children playing there. He said 'This is my garden.' He banned them and built a wall right round the garden.

The children had nowhere to play.

Winter ended and the Spring came, but it did not come to the giant's garden. There it remained Winter permanently. The seasons passed it by. The giant could not understand what had happened. The years passed. One morning he was lying in bed, shivering. He heard birdsong. He jumped out of bed and ran to the window, looking out he saw that the children had crawled through the hole in the wall and Spring had come again to the garden. The giant realized his mistake, knocked down the wall and thereafter allowed the children to play in the garden.

2 Rewrite the story.
Begin like this.

The children of the village had nowhere to play . . .

Include in the story:
- descriptions of the giant, the children, the castle and garden, and the seasons.
- descriptions of the feelings of the giant and the children at different stages of the story.
- any appropriate linking words on page 85 of appendix 3 in this workbook.

6 Pronunciation of the possessive 's'

The pronunciation of the possessive s is the same as for a plural ending.

Peter's /z/
John's /z/
Philip's /s/
Steph's /s/
George's /ɪz/
Alice's /ɪz/

Put the words in italics in the correct column, according to the pronunciation of the possessive s.

a *month's* holiday
Jane's dog
the *horse's* mouth
Joe's ambition
Uncle *Toby's* house
Mr *Walsh's* car
Beth's doll
the *judge's* decision

Liz's mother
the *Jones's* children
the *government's* duty
the *boys'* father
the *world's* resources
a *wasp's* nest
a *week's* pay

/z/	/s/	/ɪz/

7 Sentence stress

Match a question or statement in column **A** with a response in column **B**.
The part of the sentence that is stressed is in italics.

A	B
a. I hear Anne's just bought a second-hand Volvo Estate.	1 Anne's got a *brand-new Volvo estate*.
b. What kind of car has Anne got?	2 Anne's got a *brand-new* Volvo estate.
c. I like Anne's brand-new Volvo saloon.	3 Anne's got a brand new Volvo *estate*.
d. What nationality is she?	4 I *thought* she was German.
e. John said she was German.	5 *I* thought she was *German*.
f. Frank said Heidi was Swiss.	6 I thought she was *German*.
g. Congratulations! I hear you married Anne's sister last week.	7 *I'm* going to marry Anne's sister!
h. Congratulations! I hear you're going to marry Anne.	8 I'm going to marry Anne's *sister*!
i. I've just proposed to Anne's sister.	9 I'm *going* to marry Anne's sister!
j. What kind of novels do you like?	10 I *like* reading romantic novels.
k. Why do you read such rubbish?	11 I like reading *romantic novels*.
l. What do you like reading?	12 I like reading *romantic* novels.
m. He never speaks a word of truth.	13 I could tell *he* was lying.
n. What did you think of what he said?	14 I could *tell* he was lying.
o. What did you think of what they said?	15 I could tell he was *lying*.

Vocabulary

8 Words to do with light

Write one of the following words in its correct form in each space. Sometimes more than one word is possible.

shine   twinkle
dazzle   glow
flicker   sparkle
flare   flash

Literal meaning

a. '_____, _____, little star' is a well-known nursery rhyme. It means the light of the star changes rapidly from bright to faint.

b. If car drivers don't dip their headlights at night, they can _____ you, and you can't see anything.

c. This is what the dying embers of a fire do.

_____

d. Sailors who are in difficulty fire these into the air to attract attention. _____

e. This is what lightning does. _____

f. This is what the sun does. _____

g. This is what diamonds do, or the sea on a bright, clear day. _____

h. A candle _____ in a breeze, and casts shadows round a room.

Metaphorical meaning

i. The book got a _____ review in the newspaper, so I went out and bought it.

j. He's not much good at creative thinking, but he really _____ at anything that requires manual dexterity.

k. People say that just before death, the whole of your life _____ in front of you.

l. He prepared a gourmet meal, totally unassisted, in the _____ of an eye.

m. Violence has _____ up again on the island of Kroana, where the situation is bordering on civil war.

n. As soon as I saw her come on stage, I was _____ both by her beauty and performance.

o. When our eyes met, a _____ of recognition crossed his face, but he made no other sign that he remembered me.

p. The party was alright, but it lacked _____. There was nothing very exciting or lively about it.

Tick the boxes to show the differences between the words to do with light. The first one has been done for you.

	bright	dim	on and off	suddenly
sparkle	✓		✓	
shine				
glow				
twinkle				
flicker				
flare				
flash				
dazzle				

9 Homonyms

In the sentences below, the words in italic are homonyms. If you do not already understand their meanings as used here, look them up in a dictionary. Then think of, or find, at least one other meaning for each homonym.

a. Eggs are so versatile! You can boil them, fry them or *poach* them.
b. You can make them into omelettes or even *scramble* them.
c. How do you *rate* his performance? Do you think he's playing well or not?
d. Your plan certainly has my *seal* of approval. I think it's a wonderful idea.
e. The consequences of this action are *grave* and long-lasting.
f. Don't talk to me about money. It's a *tender* subject at the moment.
g. The whole argument about violence in sport *bores* me to death.
h. Ever since her accident, she's walked with a *limp*.
i. What have you *found*? Can I have a look?
j. There's a *tap* running in the bathroom. Could you turn it off?

10 Gap filling — 'The Goddess of Love'

Here is an extract from a Barbara Cartland novel, *The Goddess of Love*, with fifteen gaps.
Write one suitable word in each gap.

Corena came down the stairs, (a) _____a little tune to herself. It was a lovely day with the (b) _____sunshine lighting the daffodils under the trees. The first butterflies were (c) _____over the lilac bushes. She had no idea that she looked like a spring flower herself. she was wearing a gown which matched the sprouting buds. Her eyes, touched with gold, were the translucent green of the stream at the bottom of the garden.

She was wishing that her father was with her. He would doubtless have (d) _____ a Greek Ode which would illustrate his appreciation of the beauty she was seeing better than she could (e) _____ in words. However, not surprisingly, Sir Priam Melville was in Greece. Ever since going up to Oxford, Sir Priam had had an (f) _____ about Greece. His outstanding and unusual (g) _____ of Greek antiquity had gained him a First. Sir Priam had a Greek grandmother, so his feeling for Greece was not only in his brain but in his (h) _____.

He had then begun to collect the statues and other (i) _____ of Greece which embellished the beautiful Elizabethan house in which they dwelt. It was (j) _____ that his daughter, when she was born, should be given a Greek name. Also that she would grow up to look even more beautiful than the Greek statues which both her father and mother found entrancing.

Then, two years ago, Lady Melville had died. Corena had tried to look after her father, but she knew the only thing that would really help him to get over his (k) _____ was to be in Greece. He had told her after Christmas that that was where he was going. She thought she was lucky he had not wished to leave earlier. She was lonely without him, but her Governess, a very intelligent woman, kept her (l) _____. They (m) _____over the books that filled Sir Priam's Library, and the inscriptions which had been sent to him not long before he left. It was these inscriptions which had finally decided him he could stay away no longer from the land that enthralled him. He had (n) _____ off, looking, Corena thought, ten years younger at the (o) _____ idea of what lay ahead.

11 Matching

Match the first line of a dialogue in column **A** with the second line in column **B**.

What exactly is each dialogue about? Underline all the multi-word verbs.

A	B
a. They've laid off another 500 at Vauxhall.	1 It was in a pile of old letters in my grandfather's attic.
b. What a lovely day!	2 I sounded him out but he wasn't interested.
c. That's the third time this week the Harrods' delivery van's been at their door!	3 That's dreadful! Industry in this town may as well pack up altogether!
d. Maybe Jack'll come in on the deal.	4 Never! I look on the lot of them with profound suspicion.
e. He said it was a good buy because, despite its age, it has only 40,000 on the clock.	5 What a tragedy! To be counted out in the first round.
f. With those looks and at her age she'll be the perfect Juliet!	6 Yes, it's turned out nice again.
g. You should have voted, it's your duty.	7 I know. I really shouldn't have left out the January sales figures.
h. Actually we need about £10,000, paying it back over 3 years.	8 I know — they must have come into a fortune.
i. How did you come by the Penny Black?	9 She's having you on! She's forty if she's a day!
j. He's been knocked out! No — he's on his feet again! No — he's passed out completely.	10 You didn't fall for that old trick, did you? I bet he'd turned it back.
k. They won't like your report. You've really slipped up this time.	11 No problem, Mr Spencer. Since you branched out into mail order, it all looks very healthy indeed.

a. ___ b. ___ c. ___ d. ___ e. ___ f. ___ g. ___ h. ___ i. ___ j. ___ k. ___

12 Separable or inseparable?

Complete the following sentences twice, first with the noun phrase and then with the pronoun, making sure that the word in brackets is in the right place.

a. The management laid (off) | one hundred workers. / them.

_____

b. She came (into) | the necklace / it | when her aunt died.

_____

c. I've always looked (on) | John / him | with great respect.

_____

d. Before you make a decision, sound (out) | Mary / her | about it.

e. How did you come (by) | such a valuable picture / it | so cheaply?

_____

f. How could you fall (for) | that lie? / it?

_____

g. You must invite everybody. You can't leave (out) | Tom. / one.

_____

Three of the above multi-word verbs are type 2, which means the adverb can move when followed by a noun. Which three are they?

UNIT 9

Relative clauses

1 Defining and non-defining relative clauses (1)

As the name suggests, defining relative clauses define the noun they refer to. If we *already* clearly know which noun (in either the singular or the plural) is being described, then it cannot be followed by a defining relative clause.

The following sentences are wrong.

* *The Pope that is much respected comes from Poland.*
* *Mr Smith you met yesterday is a computer salesman.*
* *The Pacific Ocean I sailed across last year is the world's largest ocean.*

Say if the gaps in the following sentences are more likely to be filled with defining or non-defining relative clauses, or whether both are possible.

a. I don't like having to talk to people _____ .

b. Peter Smith _____ rang you earlier.

c. Politicians _____ are a dishonorable bunch of people.

d. I'll show you the photographs _____ .

e. The Houses of Parliament _____ stand on the River Thames.

f. My children _____ are coming with us on a trip to America.

g. I gave her a piece of cake _____ .

h. I'd like you to meet someone _____ .

i. The British police _____ are highly trained.

j. My cat _____ is getting a little overweight.

k. My cat's name is Wally. The only food _____ is the most expensive brand.

l. He's a very happy cat. Dogs _____ are his only source of worry in the world.

2 Defining and non-defining relative clauses (2)

Below are the missing relative clauses, without the pronouns. Put them into the correct sentence in exercise 1, inserting a relative pronoun and commas where necessary.
Some of the clauses could be either defining or non-defining, with a change in meaning. Which are they?

a. . . . were built between 1840 and 1857 . . .
b. . . . she ate greedily . . .
c. . . . I've never met before . . .
d. . . . I took on my last holiday . . .
e. . . . I've been wanting to introduce you to for ages . . .
f. . . . he eats . . .
g. . . . deceive the public . . .
h. . . . likes to sleep in front of the fire all day . . .

57

i. . . . carry guns . . .
j. . . . still go to school . . .
k. . . . chase cats . . .
l. . . . lives in Bradford, not the one who lives in Chester . . .

3 Correcting mistakes

In the following sentences, there are mistakes in the relative clauses. Find them and correct them.

a. A man to whom I was talking to recently told me a joke, which was very funny, but that I have unfortunately forgotten.
b. Our director for who's job I applied when the previous director left, has announced that the pay rise, which we asked for, has had to be postponed, that really upset us.
c. The actress Joan Kelly whose most famous film was *One for the Road* for that she won an Oscar award, has died at the age of 77 at her home in California, in which she had lived for the last twenty-five years.
d. This morning, I got a cheque in the post that I wasn't expecting, for some work, which I did a long time ago, translating business texts.
e. Lord Brown on whom many people look as the best prime minister of the century and who's memoirs that were published last year caused a scandal, got married today to a woman, who he first met fifty-five years ago, when they were at school together.

4 Spoken versus written style

Turn the following example of spoken English into more formal written English, incorporating relative clauses where appropriate. The beginning has been done for you.

'My wife and I have just had a holiday. Your agency organized it, and I feel I must complain about it. In the brochure — you sent us a brochure — it said our hotel was a stone's throw from the beach. This isn't true. In fact it's three miles from the sea, and you have to cross a motorway! Cars and lorries travel at over eighty miles an hour on it! And the swimming pool — it was shown in the picture, and it looked very inviting — doesn't exist. It is a big hole in the ground, and my children fell and cut themselves in it.

Now, then, the food. When we came to see you, you told us about the wonderful food, but it wasn't of an internationally high standard, and you promised it would be. Dinner was the same every night, and we had to wait three hours for it, and it consisted of stale bread, watery soup and cold rice.

I feel your company owes us an apology. After all, its motto is 'We aim to please'. A refund of five hundred pounds would be an acceptable amount. This was half the cost of the holiday.'

My wife and I have just had a holiday which your agency organized, and which . . .

Participles

5 Participle clauses (1)

Participle clauses can express the following ideas:

- at the same time
- because
- after
- so that/with the result that
- if

Which of the above ideas do the following participle clauses express?

a. He strolled down the road, singing a song.
b. Kissing her husband goodbye, she went off to catch the train.
c. Having spent all our money gambling, we went home.
d. Having spent all our money gambling, we couldn't afford to get a taxi home.
e. He stormed out of the house, swearing that he would never come back.
f. Knowing how much I liked grapes, she bought me a huge bunch.
g. Being a supporter of the socialist party, I am totally against private health care.
h. Having read the book, I went to bed.
i. Having read the book, I knew all about the subject.
j. She spilt wine on my suit, completely ruining it.
k. Rubbed in three times a day, Trugrow will soon have your hair growing again.
l. Outside the office, workmen were using pneumatic drills, giving us all headaches.
m. In 1986, she worked nearly eighteen hours a day, earning enough to pay off all her creditors.
n. Diagnosed early enough for treatment to take effect, measles is not a dangerous illness.

6 Participle clauses (2)

Rewrite the sentences, using one of the following words and a participle clause with **-ing**.

while   when   after   by   on   since

a. He finished work and went home.
b. He read a book and ate his supper.
c. He worked hard and saved a lot of money.
d. I came to live in the country a few years ago. I now realize how much I hated living in town.

e. He graduated from university, and went off to work in Australia.

f. When you go abroad, it is advisable to take out travel insurance.

g. I came across a wonderful book. I was browsing in our local bookshop.

h. I worked hard, and I managed to pass all my exams.

i. When you open a tin, be careful not to cut yourself.

j. When we heard the weather forecast, we decided not to go camping in the mountains.

7 Present and past participles

In the following pairs of sentences, the same verb is missing twice, once used as a present participle and once as a past participle.

Decide what you think the verb should be, and insert it in its correct form.

a. Books _____ out of the library must be returned within three weeks.

People _____ books out which haven't been stamped will be banned.

b. The film, _____ by Stephen Spielberg, is expected to be a great hit.

Power stations _____ enough energy to supply several towns are soon to be built on the south coast.

c. Crops _____ under glass mature more quickly that those in the open.

Farmers _____ such crops can therefore catch the early markets.

d. I stared at the canvas for ages, _____ the artist's skill and eye for detail.

Swiss watches, _____ for their elegance and precision, are sold throughout the world.

e. The escaped prisoner, _____ hiding in a barn, was today taken back to prison.

Many old people, _____ that their savings have been eaten into by inflation, are having difficulty in making ends meet.

f. I fell on the ice, _____ my arm.

Three people, _____ when their car crashed on the M1, were taken to hospital.

g. Whales, _____ for their valuable oil and meat, are in grave danger of extinction.

Thousands of people went shopping in the sales today, _____ for a bargain.

h. People _____ to work on the A267 from Stafford to Blaby should beware of roadworks just outside Beaton where there are hold-ups.

The first train, _____ by steam, was called Stephenson's Rocket.

i. There was a robbery at Simpson's the jeweller's today. Police are looking for a man _____ going into the shop just before the robbery took place.

You can pay the bill, _____ that you're the one with all the money.

j. We took a short-cut, _____ three hours on our journey time.

A baby _____ from drowning by a quick-thinking teenager is making good progress, and will be allowed home soon.

Writing

8 Describing a flat

A friend of yours has asked you to look around for a suitable flat. Based on the estate agent's description (and your imagination), write a report for your friend, stating the advantages and disadvantages of this particular accommodation.

WILKINS HAWSON
Estate Agents

ST. CHRISTOPHER COURT, LOWER ROAD, HILLINGDALE

The accommodation
Entrance hall - with cupboard space
Lounge - 15 × 20 Windows on two sides, with radiators, power points and imitation gas 'log' fire. A room that with little effort would become welcoming and relaxing.
Dining room - 10 × 15 A delightful room with windows overlooking the rear garden.
Kitchen - 10 × 10 Fully fitted, with oven/hob, dishwasher and ample cupboard space. A breakfast bar runs down one wall.
Bedroom 1 - 15 × 18 A large, airy room that would easily accommodate a double bed and wardrobe, with a window overlooking the rear. Bright and fresh.
Bedroom 2 - 10 × 12 An attractive guest room, or a lovely room for a single bed.
Bathroom - 12 × 12 Bath, bidet and WC in avocado green. Automatic air-extractor

There is a communal garden to the rear, which is mature and spacious. Rear garages are available to purchase.

Price: £160,000
tel: 01-776-9008

59

9 A poem – 'Flatearther'

Here is a poem where every other line is in phonemic script. Work out the words and write them in the space.

It is about an Irishman called Sean (pronounced /ʃɔːn/), who wants to prove that the earth is flat.

Flatearther

Cried Uncle Sean, 'The earth is flat!
/aɪ rɪəlɪ jæm kwaɪt ʃʊər əv ðæt/

_____

And just to prove I tell it true
/aɪl wɔːk frəm hɪə tə kætmændu:/

_____

Somewhere the earth is bound to stop,
/ðen ɒf ðɪ jedʒ aɪl ʃʊəlɪ drɒp/

_____

He left at five and got as far
/əz dʌblɪn beɪ jən mɪkɪz bɑː/

_____

'Twas five to twelve he staggered out,
/rɒkɪŋ ən riːlɪŋ ɔːl əbaʊt/

_____

At sea-wall's edge his feet they tripped
/ən daʊn əpɒn ðə biːtʃ hɪ flɪpt/

_____

He lay there thinking he was dead,
/ðen traɪjʌmf flæʃt ɪntuː hɪs hed/

_____

'I'm right! I'm right!' yelled Uncle Sean
/rɪmuːvɪŋ frəm hɪz bɪəd ə prɔːn/

_____

Which proves that when one's had some drinks,
/wʌn kæn bɪliːv djʌst wɒt wʌn θɪŋks/

_____

Jack Rendle

10 Crossword puzzle

Here is another crossword for you to try!

ACROSS

1 The surname of a nineteenth century English novelist. He wrote *Far from the Madding Crowd* (5)
4 Not poetry (5)
10 A play with music in which most of the words are sung (5)
11 Another word for a certificate (7)
12 If a place or event is this, there is great disorder and confusion because things have not been organized properly (8)
13 Your kith and --- are your relatives (3)
15 Undamaged, unbroken, for example, 'Archaeologists have found a dinosaur skeleton ------' (6)
17 Container for money (6)
19 The pound, or the franc, or the lira is a ---- of currency (4)
20 Information in response to something, for example, a survey. Consumers might give this to a producer (8)
23 A policeman wears one but a detective doesn't (7)
24 Frequently (5)
25 What you carry your arm in if you've broken or injured it (5)
26 Very strange, for example, a person or a dream. You had it in Unit 3 of the Student's book! (5)

DOWN

2 The central part of a Roman amphitheatre, for games and fights (5)
3 Disadvantage (8)
5 Thick cord, thicker and stronger than string (4)
6 What a swimmer can put in his/her mouth to breathe

with their head under water (7)

7 A word for easily noticed, for example, I felt ---------- wearing such silly clothes in the street (11)

8 Did a sum (5)

9 Extremely careful, for example ---------- research (11)

14 Good-looking (8)

16 Petty, unimportant (7)

18 Thick bars of wood used to support a ceiling. In Elizabethan houses you find a lot of these (5)

21 The table in a church or temple (5)

22 What a woman wears to a ball, or what a graduate wears at graduation (4)

11 Idioms − key words

The following sentences all contain an idiom with one key word missing. Choose one of the four alternatives to complete the idiom.

a. He used the business profits to _____ his own nest. His employees gained nothing.
fill feather enrich build

b. She's so quick to criticize other people. I think she should learn to set her own _____ in order first.
home business house place

c. He paid an absolute fortune for a really tiny flat. There's not enough room to swing a _____.
cat handbag monkey rope

d. Don't be so impatient. You can't hurry the decorating if you want to do it well. _____ wasn't built in a day.
New York St Paul's Rome Colossus

e. Friends may let you down, but your family will always stand by you. Blood is thicker than _____.
tea wine tears water

f. My car has just about had it. It's on its last _____. We'll have to get a new one.
legs life way routes

g. Politics is a cut-throat business where your friends can be more treacherous than your enemies, but, as they say, 'If you can't stand the heat, stay out of the _____.'
forge kitchen hearth desert

h. I don't know what she's got to be so cocky and self-important about. Someone should put her in her _____.
place boots cradle post

i. The wining, dining and gambling had to stop when he lost his job. He really had his _____ clipped.
tail nails claws wings

j. I believed him! He looked so sincere. I feel such a fool now. He really led me up the _____.
river garden path wrong road high street

12 Dependent Prepositions

Write the correct prepositions in each gap.

Home sweet home

Some people are indifferent (a) _____ their surroundings. They seem quite satisfied (b) _____ simply having a roof over their head and being safe (c) _____ the elements. My surroundings are very important (d) _____ me, and I like to have my possessions arranged nicely around me. I have a reputation (e) _____ being able to make any room (f) _____ a home (g) _____ home. Not that I'm obsessed (h) _____ tidiness or own anything valuable. It's a question (i) _____ being able to create a homely, comfortable atmosphere. Many people compliment me (j) _____ this. Once, however, I shared a flat (k) _____ someone who was noted (l) _____ his untidiness. He simply didn't care (m) _____ his surroundings. He dropped ash from his cigarettes, doing untold damage (n) _____ the carpet; he never made his bed, and there was no chance (o) _____ his ever doing the washing up. The dishes stood (p) _____ piles beside the sink. I tried to reason (q) _____ him, but he always had an excuse (r) _____ not doing anything. The only thing he was particular (s) _____ was his appearance. He spent hours preening himself in front of the mirror. There is a limit (t) _____ my patience. I am much happier living (u) _____ my own again.

UNIT 10

Inversion to express emphasis

1 Emphatic patterns

Rewrite the following sentences, inverting the subject and the verb. Use one of the patterns on page 144 of the Grammar section in the Student's Book.

a. I will never allow myself to be deceived in such a manner again.
b. She didn't think for one minute that she would win the competition.
c. One rarely finds a person of such integrity as Henry.
d. World peace will not be secure until all nuclear weapons are eliminated.
e. Sentries aren't allowed to leave their posts at any time.
f. Policemen are allowed to use guns only after several years' training.
g. I couldn't persuade her in any way to see the foolishness of her plan.
h. His drug problem was his downfall. He lost his job, and his wife left him, too.
i. As soon as I settled down to read the paper, the doorbell rang.
j. She little realized how the evening was to end.
k. If you ever need any help, just give me a ring.
l. If she had found out that he had been married before, she would never have married him. (Two possibilities)
m. If life on other planets were ever found, there would probably be no means of communication.

2 Making a text more emphatic

Read the advertisement, which sounds rather dull. Rewrite it to make it sound more emphatic and interesting.

THE NEW PANAMA 3000

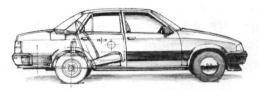

You won't appreciate the elegance of the new Panama 3000 until you get behind the steering wheel. When it comes to handling and performance, we've virtually cornered the market. You will find that the ride is the smoothest you've ever had, and you will hardly hear the engine because of the soundproofing we've installed. You will rarely have experienced such luxury whilst travelling at over 100 mph. We suggest you take a test drive, and experience the sensation yourself.

3 Writing an advertisement

Write short texts to accompany the following advertisements, including emphatic structures where appropriate.

PRINCESS COURT

The City's favourite out-of-town Rendezvous

Welcomes VIP Conferences

An exclusive Haven for discerning Executives of Major Corporations. Select residential Conferences or important Meetings, away from the Office. Exceptional Cuisine, quiet Luxury and Privacy.

Obviously
ALLCROFT

Pronouns – 'one', 'you', and 'they'

4 Referring to people impersonally

One, **they**, and **you** can sometimes be used to replace the passive, but they are not interchangeable. Usually one of the forms is more appropriate or more correct. **You** is informal, **one** is formal, and **they** is often used to mean 'those in authority'.

Make the passive verbs in the following sentences into the active, adding **one**, **they**, or **you** as the subject – whichever is the most appropriate.

a. The price of petrol has been put up again.
b. These bulbs should be planted in the autumn.
c. The flying time between London and New York has been cut by forty minutes.
d. The Queen should always be addressed as 'ma'am' or 'your majesty'.
e. A visa is needed to enter the United States.
f. Gloves and hat must be worn to the garden party.
g. Fresh herbs are required for this recipe.
h. I'd never have bought the house if I'd known a motorway was going to be built at the bottom of the garden.
i. Most children are vaccinated against measles these days.
j. Decent shoes can't be got these days.
k. Decent shoes aren't made these days.
l. A nuclear war is a calamity which, it is hoped, will never occur.

Writing

5 A formal letter

In the following letter, select the item that is more formal.

Dear Mr Henderson				

It is with regret / We are sorry | that we have to | inform / tell | you that your

phone has been | cut off, / disconnected, | because you didn't pay / due to the non-payment of | your

phone bill. We have | made every effort / tried our best | to | work out / establish | a

means whereby / way in which | you | pay / settle | the bill in instalments. | If you had / Had you

answered our | enquiries, / letters, | alternative / other | arrangements might have

been considered to | enable you to keep / let you keep | your phone, | because / since

we are generally most unwilling / we don't usually like | to | do this thing. / take this measure. | However,

we | got / received | no reply. | So / Consequently,

we have no alternative but to / there is nothing else we can do but | close / terminate | your account. We

intend to / are going to | put / place | the matter in the hands of our solicitors.

However, | if you can / should you find yourself able to | rectify the situation, / put the situation right,

we would be | happy / pleased | to hear from you. We

are anxious that you have / want you to have | your phone | reinstalled / back | as soon as possible.

A great deal of inconvenience is / Lots of problems are | avoided if bills are paid | on time. / promptly.

Yours sincerely,
James Watt, Accounts Division

6 Writing a letter of complaint and explanation

Write a reply to Mr Watt's letter.

You have not paid the phone bill because you think it does not show the right amount. It was three times the usual total. You contacted Mrs Beaton of Customer Services, who said no action would be taken until your complaint had been investigated. Ask Mr Watt to contact her. You want the matter rectified as soon as possible. Say why. Ask to have your phone reconnected, and say that you hope you do not have to pay the twenty-pound reconnection charge.

The following phrases might be useful.

I was most surprised/upset to find . . .
I would like to point out . . .
The reason I have not . . .
She assured me that she had the matter in hand.
I would be grateful if . . .
I trust that . . .

Vocabulary

7 Adverb and verb collocations

In the following sentences, one adverb goes more naturally with the verb than the other two. Underline the correct adverb.

a. I **strongly/greatly/firmly** recommend that you consider the matter carefully before making a decision.

b. I **totally/greatly/seriously** appreciate all that you've done for me.

c. Sometimes, I **deeply/totally/seriously** wonder what we're all doing here.

d. I feel very **fully/strongly/firmly** about the role of women in society.

e. I **completely/distinctly/entirely** forgot all about his birthday.

f. The government has stated quite **seriously/fully/categorically** that it intends to pursue this course of action.

g. The city was **absolutely/totally/fully** destroyed by the earthquake.

h. I sympathize most **sincerely/totally/completely** with your point of view.

i. He presented a strong case, but I wasn't **deeply/greatly/entirely** convinced that all his facts were right.

j. I **absolutely/completely/sincerely** adore ice-cream.

k. The cause of the accident will be **entirely/greatly/fully** investigated.

l. I **freely/seriously/deeply** intend to go into politics when I leave school.

8 Adverb and adjective collocations

Put a suitable intensifying adverb into each gap. Sometimes there will be several possibilities.

A Hello! I'm (a) _____ sorry I'm late. The traffic was (b) _____ awful.

B That's alright. How are you?

A (c) _____ exhausted! How about you?

B Yes, I feel (d) _____ tired myself. How did you find the exam? I thought it was (e) _____ difficult.

A Did you? I thought it was (f) _____ easy. The last question was (g) _____ obvious.

B I thought that was (h) _____ impossible! How did Alice find it?

A Well, she came out looking (i) _____ pleased with herself. She was (j) _____ convinced before the exam that she was going to fail it, but she worked (k) _____ hard in the last few weeks.

B I was (l) _____ surprised by the first question. It took me a long time to understand it. I'm (m) _____ terrified that I misunderstood it.

A Never mind. We get the results (n) _____ soon, so you'll find out then. What shall we do tonight? There's a film on that's supposed to be (o) _____ hilarious. Would you like to see it?

B That's a(n) (p) _____ great idea! I'm also (q) _____ hungry. What about you?

A I'm (r) _____ famished! Let's go!

9 Antonyms

One opposite of *poor* is, of course, *rich*, but this is only one meaning of poor. The opposite of *a poor diet* is *a balanced diet*; the opposite of *poor quality* is *high quality*.

Put in the **opposite** of the following adjectives. Choose from the list at the bottom.

a. rich food   _____ food

   rich colour   _____ colour

b. vain attempt   _____ attempt

   vain person   _____ person

c. calm sea   _____ sea

   calm person   _____ person

d. stiff breeze   _____ breeze

   stiff punishment   _____ punishment

e. bright light   _____ light

   bright student   _____ student

f. reasonable
   person   _____ person

   reasonable price   _____ price

g. plain wallpaper   _____ wallpaper

   plain
   architectural
   style   _____ architectural
                                  style

h. odd number   _____ number

     odd working hours   _____ working hours

i. moderate amount   _____ amount

     moderate politics   _____ politics

j. genuine diamond   _____ diamond

     genuine emotion   _____ emotion

k. flat countryside   _____ countryside

     flat road   _____ road

l. clear sky   _____ sky

     clear conscience   _____ conscience

rough	exorbitant	excessive
pale	overcast	modest/humble
dim	guilty	successful
bumpy	tense/temperamental	fake
lenient	even	insincere
irrational	regular	slow
patterned	plain	hilly/mountainous
gentle	extreme	elaborate/ornate

10 Gap filling – 'Royal Talk'

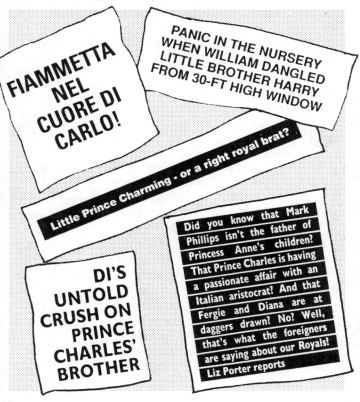

FIAMMETTA NEL CUORE DI CARLO!

PANIC IN THE NURSERY WHEN WILLIAM DANGLED LITTLE BROTHER HARRY FROM 30-FT HIGH WINDOW

Little Prince Charming - or a right royal brat?

DI'S UNTOLD CRUSH ON PRINCE CHARLES' BROTHER

Did you know that Mark Phillips isn't the father of Princess Anne's children? That Prince Charles is having a passionate affair with an Italian aristocrat? And that Fergie and Diana are at daggers drawn? No! Well, that's what the foreigners are saying about our Royals!
Liz Porter reports

Fill each gap with **one** suitable word.

> Did you know that Prince William is so uncontrollable that Prince Charles has (a) _____ him over to a disciplinarian naval officer to be "tamed"? And that a jealous Diana isn't speaking to Fergie because she recently said: "I'm doing so well - perhaps I'll be Queen of England one day?" Or that Diana's been having fertility (b) _____ , while Fergie's been contemplating an operation to get fat off her hips - and that both royal wives are in (c) _____ over the imminent break-up of their respective marriages?
>
> And what about the latest on Princess Anne's children - they really aren't Mark's you know . . .
>
> Well at least you would only know these things if you lived in Germany, where you would have gleaned them all – and more – in just one week of reading the local magazines.
>
> On the other hand, if you were resident in Italy, you'd be able to speak with some (d) _____ on the big affair between Prince Charles and the Italian aristocrat Fiammetta Frescobaldi.
>
> HRH may have managed to evade Fleet Street's nosiest newshounds, but the Italian Magazine *Novella 2000* was hot on the (e) _____. Charles, the magazine reported, has been making secret trips to Italy, usually under the (f) _____ of an art museum visit or a shooting party, when he would 'wander around Tuscan aristocrats' properties, hoping for a lucky meeting with the object of his desire.'
>
> Meanwhile in London, reporter Dea Borletti confided, 'Diana is in tears, with court gossip saying her weight (g) _____ has been due to jealousy, not illness.'Queen Elizabeth, apparently put the blame for the 'adventure' on Diana who 'should have kept a tighter (h) _____ on her husband'. When Charles hasn't been (i) _____ off to Italy, Borletti revealed, he has been writing or phoning . . . and has already put his sentiments into a poem.
>
> The article, (j) _____ DIANA IS JEALOUS, CHARLES LOVES SOMEBODY ELSE came with pictures which have managed to capture the (k) _____ lovers in the same frame, although Charles is walking paces ahead of his purported paramour - and looks as if he wishes he were home in front of *Dallas* with Di.
>
> For sheer verve and inventiveness, *Novella 2000* should take the (l) _____ for the best piece of fiction starring the Royal Family. But it still has competition from across the border.
>
> The French weekly newspaper *France Dimanche* is always a good (m) _____ of impending royal divorces. They revealed for the (n) _____ time, the 'true' story of 'Princess Anne and the handsome actor [for two years they have been inseparable]', describing how shocked the English were to see Anne sharing a box at the theatre with Anthony Andrews the day before celebrating her wedding anniversary alone . . .
>
> Where did they get these stories from? A London-based correspondent for several German magazines [who didn't want to be named] says: 'They make them up. If they've got a picture, like one of Anne with Anthony Andrews, they'll just (o) _____ the story to go with it.'

Pronunciation

11 Word stress

Many long words in English have the main stress on the third syllable from the end:

authority   oOoo
passionate   Ooo

Look at the following words from the text on 'Royal Talk'. Decide which have the stress on the third syllable from the end, and put them in the correct column. There are twelve.

Put the remaining words in the correct column according to their stress.

anniversary respective uncontrollable celebration
magazine properties imminent adventure
aristocrat inseparable (careful!) competition inventive
disciplinarian separation fertility resident
operation correspondent contemplate sentiments
museum celebrate contemplation jealousy

Third from the end	ooO	Oooo	ooOo	oOo

Multi-word verbs

12 Some multi-word verbs and their Latin-based synonyms

Many multi-word verbs have a synonym of Latin origin. The multi-word verb tends to be more informal, and the word of Latin origin tends to be more formal and literary.

Guessing meaning

Try to guess the meaning of the multi-word verbs in the following sentences.

a. I was badly **beaten up** when I tried to break up a fight outside a pub last night.
b. You should tell the police that it wasn't your fault. I'll **stick up for** you, don't worry.
c. Soon there will be no import duties within the Common Market. They're going to **do away with** them.
d. Government forces in Walliland have **put down** a revolt by a group of soldiers.
e. The business went through a lean period at the beginning of the year, but things are **picking up** now.
f. Looking after six kids all day has completely **worn** me **out**!
g. Many old people are **taken in** by bogus officials, who call at their houses, find a pretence for looking round and then steal their property.
h. I was **told off** for being late again this morning. If it happens again, my pay gets docked.
i. We've bought an old house which isn't in very good condition, but we'll **do** it **up** bit by bit.
j. Don't believe her when she says she's got stomach ache. She's **putting** it **on**. She just wants to get out of going to school.
k. I had a very unhappy childhood, but the delights of being an adult and a parent have **made up for** that.
l. I can't solve the riddle at all. I **give in**. What's the answer?
m. The government is going to **set up** an inquiry into the condition of Britain's prisons.
n. Police have **ruled out** murder, but are still holding several people for questioning.
o. He's a great mate of mine. He's the kind of friend who'll **stand by** you through thick and thin.

Matching

Match one of the above multi-word verbs with its Latin synonym.

1 _____ compensate for
2 _____ exhaust
3 _____ deceive
4 _____ defend
5 _____ pretend
6 _____ abolish
7 _____ reprimand
8 _____ suppress
9 _____ establish
10 _____ exclude
11 _____ improve
12 _____ decorate
13 _____ surrender
14 _____ support
15 _____ assault

UNIT 11

Hypothesizing

1 Expressing wishes

Respond to the following facts with a wish.

a. My eldest son isn't very bright.

   I wish he _____

b. You worry too much.

   I wish you _____

c. I overslept this morning and I was late for work.

   If only _____

d. She's desperately shy.

   If only _____

e. I don't want you to drive so far in one day.

   I'd rather _____

f. I've been given the sack!

   If only _____

g. I want you to settle down and get a decent job.

   It's time _____

h. He won't apologize for breaking it.

   I wish _____

i. She drank too much at the party.

   She wishes _____

j. I really want to give up smoking.

   If only _____

k. My father didn't want me to marry Jim.

   He'd rather _____

l. I had to lie to her.

   If only _____

m. Everybody except us has a word processor these days.

   It's about time _____

n. He couldn't complete it on time.

   He wishes _____

o. She had her hair cut really short.

   She wishes _____

2 Contrasting wishes with facts

Complete the following hypothetical statements with a short factual comment.

I wish I weren't hard-up all the time but I am

a. I wish I earned more but _____

b. If only I had listened but _____

c. If only I had a better typewriter but _____

d. If only I hadn't been made redundant but _____

e. I wish he wouldn't criticize me all the time but _____

f. I wish we'd left earlier but _____

g. I wish he would leave but _____

h. If only you'd been more thorough but _____

i. If only she'd had more time but _____

j. She wishes he would remember their anniversary but _____

k. If only she loved me but _____

l. They wish they knew the answer but _____

3 Tense usage for fact and non-fact (1)

Put the verb in brackets in an appropriate tense to express either fact or non-fact. Where there is no verb _ _ _, insert an auxiliary verb.

A I wish we (a) _____ (not have) to go out

tonight, but we have no choice. I (b) _____ (like) to stay in and watch the film on television. If only we (c) _ _ _! If only your boss

(d) _____ (not invite) us!

B I know, but it's important. It (e) _____

(be) alright if he (f) _____ (not go) on and on about how wonderful his children are, but he always (g) _ _ _. He talks as if they

(h) _____ (be) angels, but they

(i) _____ always _____ (misbehave).

A Listen! Suppose we (j) _____ (ring) them

and (k) _____ (say) that we (l) _____ (break) down on the way there. That's a good excuse, isn't it?

B No, I'd rather we (m) _____ (go). Don't

worry. It (n) _____ (not last) for long.

Just look as though you (o) _____ (enjoy) yourself.
A All right. Sorry.

4 Tense usage for fact and non-fact (2)

Put the verb in brackets in an appropriate tense or verb form.

A Hello, dear. Have a nice day at the office?
B No.

A You look as if you (a) _____ (can) do with a drink. What's the matter?
B It's Annie at the office. She acts as though she

(b) _____ (be) the only one who

(c) _____ (do) any work. She (d)

_____ always _____ (go on) about *her* sales record, and how many business

machines *she* (e) _____ (sell) this month.

So I told her what I (f) _____ (think) of her today.

A Oh dear! I (g) _____ (not do) that. I think

I (h) _____ (try) to be a bit more diplomatic. How did she take it?

B She blew up.

A I (i) _____ (love) (j) _____ (see)

her face when you (k) _____ (tell) her!

B I (l) _____ (not mind) if she just (m)

_____ (listen) to other people sometimes! And she's always telling us about where she goes and what she does in the evening. As if it

(n) _____ (matter)! It's all *her* wonderful home and *her* wonderful husband!
A Yes, and from what I've heard, it's not as though

she (o) _____ (have) much to boast about!

What if you all (p) _____ (ignore) her?

Do you think that (q) _____ (work)?
B No.
A How much does she earn? Twenty thousand a year?
B I (r) _____ (not think) she (s) _____

(earn) as much as that, judging by the way she

dresses. She looks as though she (t) _____ (get) all her clothes from jumble sales.
A Is the office busy at the moment?
B Terribly. I was given three new projects today.

As if I (u) _____ (not have) enough to do

already! I (v) _____ (like) (w) _____ turn them down, but I had to accept them.

A You sound as though things (x) _____ (get) you down at the moment.
B You can say that again!

Present subjunctive

5 Transforming to a 'that' clause

The verbs in the following sentences are followed either by an **-ing** form or an infinitive. Rewrite the sentences to include a **that** clause. In some cases you will need to use the present subjunctive or **should**.

a. I insist on her telling me the truth.
b. He promised to come on time.
c. I admit telling you lies.
d. He recommended having the trout. So I did.
e. I propose setting another date for the meeting. Do we agree?
f. I am asking you to allow him to go free.
g. The king ordered his followers to raise an army.
h. 'I suggest getting an early night,' I said to my son, who was yawning.
i. I complained about the cold food and the bad service

j. I am convinced of his honesty.
k. The company requests visitors to fill in a name tag.
l. I command every citizen to swear allegiance to me.

Review of tenses and verb forms

6 Producing the correct tenses and verb forms

Put the verb in brackets into the correct tense or verb form.

Gunmen walk into police ambush after officers tipped off over plans

A big armed robbery (a) _____ (foil) yesterday when gunmen walked into a police ambush in central London.

The gang (b) _____ (hold up) a security van after it (c) _____ (collect) more than £600,000 from shops around the City, but they (d) _____ (not have) time to begin (e) _____ (put) their plan into operation. If it (f) _____ (succeed), it (g) _____ (be) one of the largest this year.

However, the gang's carefully planned raid (h) _____ (betray), and police, (i) _____ (act) on a tip-off, knew where and when it (j) _____ (take) place.

Officers from the Metropolitan Police flying squad and the firearms unit set an elaborate trap.

Plain-clothes detectives (k) _____ (position) in streets and cars around the London Electricity showrooms just north of the City, where the van (l) _____ (pick) up takings. The robbers, who were armed with pistols, (m) _____ (allow) to loiter outside the showroom entrance and wait for the van to arrive.

A police spokesman refused (n) _____ (discuss) what happened next or to say how many officers (o) _____ (involve) in the operation. Witnesses said that as the raid (p) _____ (begin), plain-clothes detectives came out from a side road and used a Post Office van to block off a possible escape route down the street.

Meanwhile, marksmen who (q) _____ (hide) behind a wall in front of the showroom appeared behind the gunmen and called on them (r) _____ (surrender).

The three (s) _____ (throw) to the ground and (t) _____ (handcuff). Scotland Yard said that no shots (u) _____ (fire).

Last night three men (v) _____ (interview) at City Road Police Station. They (w) _____ (appear) in court tomorrow.

Writing

7 Nouns which add cohesion

Some nouns summarize recently given information, or point to what is to come.

Put one of the following nouns into each gap. Sometimes more than one noun is possible.

move	trend
issue	view
problem	point
situation	question
fact	

The (a) _____ of what should be done to help the long-term unemployed is one that has vexed many governments over the last fifteen years. Some think that the unemployed should move to parts of the country where there are jobs available, but this

(b) _____ is not widely shared and is very

unrealistic. The (c) _____ is that there are jobs in the prosperous South East, but people from other areas cannot afford to live there. There has been an influx of population into the South East, and this, coupled with the amount of money that people earn and a shortage of housing, has made house prices shoot up.

This (d) _____ shows no sign of abating.

The Government has tried to encourage industry to relocate by setting up regional development boards and offering generous grants, but these

(e) _____, although laudable, have had little

real effect. The (f) _____ that most politicians overlook is that being unemployed for

years on end is a soul-destroying (g) _____.

The (h) _____ is that there will never be full employment in this country again, and no government knows where best to stand on this

(i) _____.

Write two or three similar paragraphs about a political problem in your country, using where appropriate the nouns which add cohesion. Here are some more which might help you.

aspect
decision
argument
debate
conclusion
prospect

8 Rhyming pairs

Each word on the left rhymes with one word only on the right. Match the words that rhyme.

brain	deaf
teeth	great
lost	beef
foot	breath
boast	skull
suit	Les
weight	reign
slight	days
death	tossed
says	post
dull	height
phrase	wreath
war	food
full	shoot
chef	put
leaf	law
glued	wool

Try to write a short poem using some of the rhyming words.

9 Tongue twisters

Here are some well-known English tongue twisters. Try saying each one as quickly as possible.

Sister Suzie sitting on a thistle

She sells sea-shells on the sea shore.
The sea-shells that she sells are sea-shells I'm sure.

Peter Piper picked a peck of pickled pepper;
A peck of pickled pepper Peter Piper picked;
If Peter Piper picked a peck of pickled pepper,
Where's the peck of pickled pepper Peter Piper picked?

10 Slips of the tongue

Sometimes when we are under pressure, we make mistakes when we speak, and things don't quite come out as we intend! Here are some sentences spoken by television and radio presenters. Can you work out what they wanted to say?

a. . . . and how long have you had this life-long ambition?
b. Two million pounds' worth of priceless prints and paintings have been stolen.
c. Conditions on the road are bad, so if you're just setting off for work, leave a little earlier.
d. The robbery was committed by a pair of identical twins. Both are said to be aged about twenty.
e. The Conservatives' policy of non-intervention to support ailing industry is a hot potato which could leave the Government with egg all over its face.
f. We were unanimous — in fact, everyone was unanimous.
g. Of course, Kirkpatrick will serve nowhere near the nine hundred years to which he has been sentenced, because the system of parole allows for up to fifty per cent remission for good behaviour.
h. The world record is 38 seconds, and not many people have done better than that.
i. And now coming onto the court are the Gullikson twins, an interesting pair, both from Wisconsin, USA . . .
j. Finally, but by no means last . . .

11 Compound words

Make compound words according to the definitions, using the word in bold as the first word of the compound.

Use your dictionary to see if the compound is written as one word or with a hyphen, and mark the stress. Sometimes the stress is on the first word, and sometimes on the second.

out

a. _____ To be more numerous than; we say *Men*

_____ *women.*

b. _____ To gain an advantage over an opponent (perhaps at chess) by playing in a clever and skilful way.

c. _____ You are this if you give your opinions about things openly and honestly, even if they are likely to offend.

d. _____ A reaction of strong disapproval and anger shown by the public.

e. _____ The amount of something that a person or a factory makes or produces.

f. _____ A set of clothes, especially one that you wear on a special occasion.

g. _____ A person is this if they are very friendly and open in their behaviour.

h. _____ The shape of things, especially when you cannot see it clearly, and can only see its profile.

up

i. _____ To make more modern, for example, a machine or information.

j. _____ The final result of a series of events or discussions. We say *The dispute was long and bitter, but the*

_____ *was victory to the government*.

back

k. _____ A large amount of business which has accumulated over a period of time which needs to be dealt with. We say *After the postal strike, there was a*

_____ *of letters to be delivered*.

l. _____ Work is this if it requires a lot of hard, physical effort.

m. _____ If a plan or project does this, it has the opposite result to the one you wanted. We say *He plotted to discredit his superior so that he could get his job,*

but his plan _____ *when he was found out and dismissed*.

down

n. _____ The thing that causes a person to be ruined or to fail. We say *Drink was his*

_____ .

o. _____ A person is this if they are realistic and practical, and don't have their head in the clouds!

12 Pairs of words joined with 'and'

There are many pairs of words that go together, usually in a fixed order, joined by **and**.

kings and queens
knife and fork
black and blue

Complete the sentences below, filling the first gap with a word from column **A** and the second gap with a word from column **B**.

A	B
hands	cons
cut	fro
flesh	tired
facts	knees
to	seek
hide	far
odds	wide
sick	figures
pros	dried
hard	ends
by	large
few	blood
far	fast

a. How can you be so cruel to your own son? After

all, he is your own _____ and _____ .

b. Some compound nouns in English are written as one word, some as two and some are hyphenated.

There aren't any _____ and _____ rules.

c. I didn't buy much at the shops, just a few

_____ and _____ for the children.

d. I opened the door and found Mary on her

_____ and _____ looking for her contact lens.

e. I'm _____ and _____ of the noise our neighbours make! I'm going round right now to give them a piece of my mind!

f. I can't make up my mind on the question of allowing abortion. I can see both _____ and _____ .

g. I am given a very free reign in my job. _____ and _____ , I can do exactly as I want.

h. I had a game of _____ and _____ with the children. I counted to a hundred, then went to look for them, but I couldn't find them anywhere.

i. Most television output is absolute rubbish. The times when you see a genuinely interesting programme are _____ and _____ between.

j. The Azra Trading Company is considering taking over a smaller distributor, but they are looking at all the _____ and _____ before deciding.

k. There is no _____ and _____ solution to the problem of violence in our society. So many different factors have to be taken into account, and so many points of view.

l. She sat in the rocking chair, moving gently _____ and _____ , and staring into the fire.

m. He was adopted at the age of three. As an adult, he searched _____ and _____ to find his true parents, but to no avail.

13 Idioms − key words

The following sentences contain the key word of an idiom. Find the key word in your dictionary and complete the idiom.

a. The Social Democratic and Liberal Alliance did well in the 1984 elections, but this victory was just a *flash* _____ because they achieved nothing thereafter.

b. Government statistics say there are about five thousand people in this country living below the poverty line. But this, of course, is just the *tip* _____ . There are many, many more.

c. **A** We're going camping this weekend. Do you want to come with us?
   B No, thanks. Being wet through all night long and getting dirt in your food isn't exactly my *cup* _____ .

d. 'The government's economic policy is in ruins, but they won't admit it! All they talk about is spies and the need to keep state secrets, but they're using this issue as a *red* _____ _____ so no-one will ask them about the economy.'

e. **A** I'm going out with Tom this evening. Do you know him?
   B I know him, but I wouldn't _____ _____ *barge-pole*. I think he's repulsive.

f. Can you help me to build this set of drawers? I've got the instructions but I can't make *head* _____ of them.

g. She had no intention of going away on holiday, but then, on the *spur* _____ , she went into a travel agent and booked a package tour to Greece.

h. When you first start to drive, it's difficult to co-ordinate your hands and feet, but you soon _____ *hang* _____ .

i. **A** Listen! Borrow a couple of thousand pounds and come away with us.
   B Huh! That's *easier* _____ ! Where do you think I'm going to get that from?

j. **A** I can't stand David. He's absolutely stinking rich.
   B Well, I think you've got to give *credit* _____ . He did build up his business from scratch, and it took years.

14 Dependent prepositions

Write the correct preposition in each gap.

Growing older

The likelihood (a) _____ living to be a hundred has increased enormously over recent years, largely due (b) _____ improvements (c) _____ health care and diet. It seems (d) _____ me as I journey (e) _____ life that people generally seem content (f) _____ whatever age they are. Very few of my middle-aged friends think (g) _____ nostalgically to their long-gone teenage years; years fraught (h) _____ lack (i) _____ confidence, trying to establish relationships (j) _____ the opposite sex, and often (k) _____ conflict (l) _____ one's parents. No, they feel (m) _____ the prime of their life.

(n) _____ the other hand, when they look (o) _____ the future and inevitable old age, their feelings are more ambiguous. Of course they hope (p) _____ a long life, but what if suddenly, or (q) _____ degrees, there is a deterioration (r) _____ their health or mental faculties, and they become a burden (s) _____ their friends and families? No-one can insure (t) _____ such a thing happening. To be hale and hearty and a hundred years old is one thing, but to be afflicted (u) _____ all manner of aches, pains and senile wanderings of the mind is quite another.

UNIT 12

Nouns with a special meaning in the plural

1 Singular and plural nouns

Complete the pairs of sentences below with the following words. The same word is used in both sentences in each pair, once in its singular and once in its plural form.

quarter	condition
term	experience
youth	saving
good	damage
pain	honour
ground	length

a. Under the _____ of the contract, you are obliged to repay the loan within two years.

The car was a reasonable price, but wasn't in good _____.

b. It has been an _____ to work with you. I've been very proud of what we've achieved together.

She has an _____ degree in geography.

c. I have a terrible _____ at the back of my neck.

He took great _____ to ensure his guests' stay was pleasant.

d. After the accident, it took her a long time to come to _____ with the fact that she would never dance again.

During his first _____ of office, the Prime Minister made many sensible decisions.

e. We need a person with relevant _____ to fill the post.

f. He wrote a book about his _____ whilst crossing Africa on foot.

f. The Vicar was a kind man, and did a lot of _____ during his life.

There is a wide range of electrical _____ on sale in our village shop.

g. The day return fare is only £12 — a _____ of £8 on the full fare.

Mrs Higgins' house was broken into the other day, and all her _____ were taken.

h. Officers don't live with ordinary soldiers. Their _____ are usually separate and more luxurious.

Interest rates have risen to 8¼ per cent, a rise of a _____ of a per cent.

i. For some reason, he was ashamed of his working class background, and went to great _____ to conceal the fact.

I can only swim one _____ of the swimming pool before I get tired.

j. Don't sit on the grass. The _____ is still very wet.

I trust John. I have good _____ for believing his version of events.

k. The storm caused a lot of _____.

She was awarded four thousand pounds' _____ in the libel case.

l. Two _____ were seen running away from the scene of the crime.

_____ has always been the time for rebellion.

74

Articles

2 Comparing sentences

Compare the use (or absence) of articles in the following sentences.

a. Is there life after death?

   She has lived a life of misery since the death of her husband.

b. They experience freedom from pain.

   The freedom to say what you want is a basic democratic freedom.

c. There's a feeling of love, joy, beauty and peace.

   My new car's a beauty. It's a real joy to drive.

d. That numerous people have had Near Death Experiences is not in doubt.

   There is still a doubt in my mind about whether it was the right thing to do.

e. The future looks bleak – drought, disease and economic collapse.

   The drought in Africa last year cost many lives. There is a drought every year.

3 An article or not?

Write **a**, **the** or nothing in each gap.

a. _____ worry about _____ state of

   his finances drove him to _____ despair.

b. He sauntered down _____ streets without

   _____ worry in _____ world.

c. _____ main worry of _____ most

   people is _____ good health.

d. _____ news is just coming into _____

   studio of _____ fire at _____ home

   of Mr Paul Beaston, _____ film Director.

e. I can't wait to go on holiday. _____ sea,

   _____ sand and _____ books –
   that's what I want.

f. I went to _____ theatre last night and saw

   _____ great play. I thought it was good,

   anyway, but I read in _____ papers this

   morning that _____ critics had slammed it.

g. _____ Paris of _____ 1980's is

   nothing compared to _____ Paris of

   _____ 1968.

h. She was appointed _____ President of

   _____ National Union of _____
   Printworkers.

i. _____ last year was good for business.

j. _____ last year has been good for business.

k. I decorated _____ children's bedroom as

   fast as I could. In _____ week, I had
   finished.

l. I haven't got time to phone him at the week-end.

   I'll do it in _____ week.

m. I met my wife at _____ party on _____

   New Year's Eve. It was on _____
   Wednesday, I seem to recall.

Ways of adding emphasis

4 The use of '-ever' for emphasis

Write **whatever**, **whoever**, **whichever**, **whenever**, **wherever** or **however** in the gaps in the following sentences.

a. Teenagers are remarkable when it comes to

   money. _____ much you give them, it's
   never enough.

b. There are two cakes left. Take _____ one
   you want.

c. _____ you're in London, you must look
   me up.

d. Someone's taken my dictionary. _____ it
   was, could they please give it back to me.

e. The library was closed, so I had to rely on

   _____ books I had at home.

f. We have tried to restore the house _____
   possible to its original state.

g. He's always ringing up from Paris or New York

   or _____ to say how much he loves me.

h. _____ many times I'm told someone's
   name, I can never remember it.

i. I hope that _____ you vote for in the next election, you at least know why you are voting for them.

j. This is the erase button on the word processor, so _____ you do, don't touch it.

5 Revision of linking words and phrases

In the following text, one or two (but not more) of the linking words and phrases are correct, and the others are incorrect. Underline the correct ones.

123 Jalan Pandan
Singapore 9
June 23rd

Dear Mum and Dad

You must be wondering why you haven't heard from me over the last couple of weeks. (a) | Basically, Honestly, Actually, | it is | due to on account because

I've been trying to collect my thoughts (c) | so as to / to / for | find the right words to tell you what has happened. (d) | Naturally, Ideally, Surely,

I don't want anyone to feel hurt (e) | as a result of / on / following | any decision I might make.

I know I promised when I took the job here that it would be for a maximum of two years and (f) | consequently immediately after that | I would

return home and run the family business. Believe me, (g) | at that time, at the beginning, in the beginning, | that was what I genuinely planned to do.

(h) | Although But However, | two things have happened to make me want to change those plans - (i) | not only at last for one thing | have I been

offered a permanent contract, (j) | moreover but also and | I have fallen in love - with Neil, a colleague in the same department - I've

mentioned him often in letters. (k) | Personally, Anyway, Naturally, | we would like to get married out here quite soon. I do hope you both

aren't too shocked and disappointed by all of this, (l) | As well, In addition, In any case, | hasn't Paul always shown more flair for business

than me? (m) | In the main All in all In conclusion | might it not be the best solution that my baby brother run the family firm? (n) | Personally, Obviously, Eventually,

I think he'd do it very well.
Please write soon. I can't feel truly and completely happy about it all until I hear your reactions. I can't wait for you to meet Neil - I just know you'll love him!

All my love
    Kay
        xx

Pronunciation

6 A poem – 'Hints on pronunciation for foreigners'

Practise the following poem, which illustrates the irregular spelling of English.

HINTS ON PRONUNCIATION FOR FOREIGNERS

I take it you already know
Of *tough* and *bough* and *cough* and *dough*?
Others may stumble but not you,
On hic*cough*, thor*ough*, *laugh* and *through* . . .
Well done! And now you wish, perhaps,
To learn of less familiar traps.

Beware of *heard*: a dreadful word
That looks like *beard* and sounds like *bird*.
And *dead*: it's said like *bed* not *bead* –
For goodness' sake don't call it *deed*.
Watch out for *meat* and *great* and *threat*
(They rhyme with *suite* and *straight* and *debt*!)

A *moth* is not a *moth* in *mother*;
Nor *both* in *bother*, *broth* in *brother*;
And *here* is not a match for *there*,
Nor *dear* and *fear* for *bear* and *pear*.
And then there's *dose* and *rose* and *lose* –
(Just look them up) and *goose* and *choose*,
And *cork* and *work* and *card* and *ward*,
And *font* and *front* and *word* and *sword*,
And *do* and *go* and *thwart* and *cart* . . .
Come, come! I've hardly made a start.
A dreadful language? Man alive!
I'd mastered it when I was five!

I will teach you in my verse
Words like *corps*, *corks*, *horse* and *worse*.
For this phonetic labyrinth
Gives *monkey*, *donkey*, *ninth* and *plinth*;
Wounded, *rounded*, *grieve* and *sieve*;
Friend and *fiend*; *alive* and *live*.
Query does not rhyme with *very*,
Nor does *fury* sound like *bury*.
Dies and *diet*; *lord* and *word*,
Earth and *hearth* and *clerk* and *herd*;
Evil, *devil*, *tomb*, *bomb*, *comb*;
Doll, *roll*, *dull*, *bull*, *some* and *home*.
Finally - for I've said enough -
Through though thorough plough cough tough!
While *hiccough* has the sound of *cup* . . .
My advice is: GIVE IT UP!

Vowel sounds

Put the words which are either wholly or partly in italics on the correct line, according to the pronunciation of the italicized vowel sound. Some have been done for you.

/ʌ/   tough _____

/aʊ/   bough _____

/ɒ/   cough _____

/əʊ/ _____

/ə/ _____

/ɑ:/ _____

/u:/ _____

/ɜ:/ _____

/ɪə/ _____

/e/ _____

/i:/ _____

/eɪ/ _____

/eə/ _____

/ɔ:/ _____

/aɪ/ _____

/ɪ/ _____

/ʊ/ _____

Vocabulary

7 Noun collocations

Reply to the questions using one of the following countable nouns and the uncountable noun in brackets. Add any other further information if necessary.

**sheet   word   breath   plot   pinch
suit   stroke   burst   wink   hint**

a. Where did you get all that money from? (luck; horses)

_____

b. What did knights wear in medieval times to protect themselves? (armour)

_____

c. Why are you going outside? (fresh air)

_____

d. Do you need a whole pad? (no; paper)

_____

e. Does Sheila work? (no work ever in her life)

_____

f. Did your accountant help you with your problem? (yes; advice)

_____

g. You look shattered! (yes; no sleep last night)

_____

h. Did you believe what Tom said about having a yacht and a villa? (no; salt)

_____

i. Were the fans well-behaved at the football match? (yes; no trouble)

_____

j. Where's your house going to be built? (land; overlooking the sea)

_____

k. Did you see any fighting when the riot started? (gunfire; middle of the night)

_____

_____

8 Collective nouns

Match a collective noun in column **A** with an appropriate noun in column **B**.

A	B
	directors
	cards
	old clothes
	deer
a flock	sheep
a swarm	grapes
a herd	actors
a pack	thieves
a board of	drug pushers
a bunch	soldiers
a bundle	bees
a company	wolves
a gang	flowers
a ring	sticks
	lies
	cattle
	keys
	labourers

9 Gap-filling — 'My dead daughter will be recreated'

Write one suitable word in each gap.

MY DEAD DAUGHTER WILL BE RECREATED, PLEDGES FATHER

The father of a teenage girl murdered three years ago hopes to (a) _____ her back to life using a cell from her brain.

Patricia Wilson's brain was frozen hours after her (b) _____ body was found.

Now her father, American author Robert Wilson, believes scientists will be able to (c) _____ her in 10 to 15 years.

He said: 'I want to give her the (d) _____ in life that a drunken burglar took away.

'I'm sure that science will produce its first (e) _____ clone in the next few years.'

Patricia, 15 – called Luna by her family – was (f) _____ slaughtered in a San Francisco store where she worked as a part-time clerk.

Her father ordered the brain to be taken to a Californian firm that (g) _____ in freezing bodies for science.

He said: 'Cloning is so close to being (h) _____. Luna would not have her complete personality if she were brought back but she would be an (i) _____ twin in every other way.

'I believe science will find a way to (j) _____ her during my lifetime.'

Dr Paul Segall of the University of California, helped the Wilson family freeze Luna's brain.

He said: 'Her murder was a terrible (k) _____. Like Mr Wilson, I believe cloning will be possible in the next 15 years and I'll do anything to help his wish come true.

'He loved his daughter very dearly and is not asking the impossible. Thirty years ago men on the moon and (l) _____ babies were just dreams. Now we have both.'

Luna's brain is (m) _____ in chemicals and frozen at minus 320 deg F in liquid nitrogen. The brain (n) _____ can be (o) _____ alive for hundreds of years.

Mr Wilson pays £150 a year to have the brain preserved. He said: 'Doctors have (p) _____ that they can clone animals. Humans will be next – and I will do anything to get my daughter back.'

10 Crossword puzzle

Here is a final crossword for you to try!

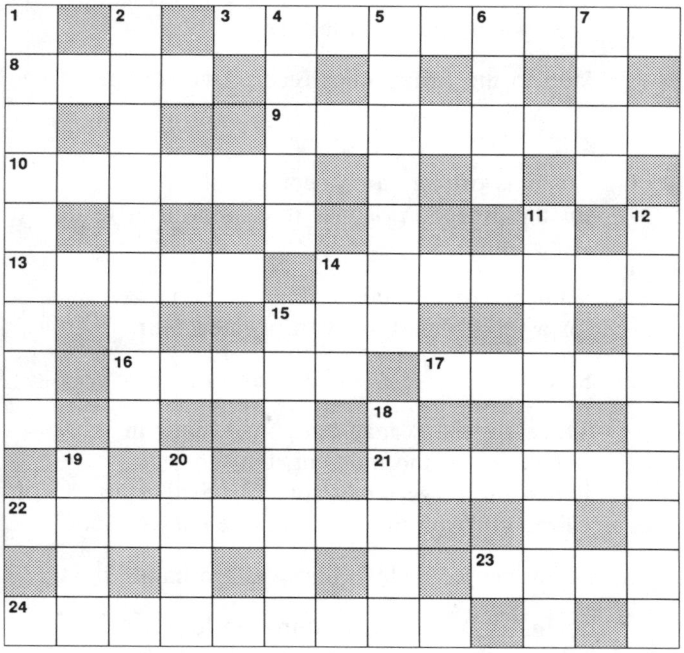

(Crossword grid)

ACROSS
3 Person who flies in a spaceship (9)
8 Hairless (4)
9 Rare (8)
10 Unpleasant and upsetting experience (6)
13 Compass point (5)
14 A person who is pleasant and easy to talk to is this —
rather a literary word (7)
15 Secret agent (3)
16 Announce; say in a formal way (5)
17 A popular game where numbers are called out and
you have to match them with a card you have in front
of you (5)
21 Oriental market (6)
22 Brown-haired girl (8)
23 Pain (4)
24 Month (9)

DOWN
1 Stubborn (9)
2 Large sea bird (9)
4 Section of a police force, for example, the drug -----
(5)
5 To put right — a formal word (7)
6 When the dentist gives you an injection, your mouth
goes ---- (4)
7 Once ---- a time (4)
11 If you have something in ---------, you have lots of it
(9)
12 Coal, iron and oil are natural --------- (9)
14 Monkey (3)
15 A layer of rock (7)
18 Extremely fat (5)
19 Liberate (4)
20 The French franc is a ---- of currency (4)

11 Multi-word verbs, and nouns formed from them

The majority of nouns consisting of a verb with a
particle do not have a corresponding multi-word verb
with the same meaning.

*Technological advances in space research have
yielded many **spin-offs** for ordinary people, for
example, non-stick saucepans.*

A **spin-off** is something useful that happens
unexpectedly as a result of activities designed to
achieve something else. There is no corresponding
verb 'to spin off'.

However, with some there is a link. A **push-up** is an
exercise where you **push up** your body.

Complete the pairs of sentences below with the
following verb-and-particle combinations. The same
combination is used in both sentences in each pair,
once as a verb and once as a noun. All the nouns
(except one) have the verb as the first element.

check up	break out	give away
write off	crack down	put down
clear out	get together	print out
look out	set up	rip off (informal)
slip up	sell out	

a. Tickets for the concert have _____. It's
impossible to buy one except from a tout.

The football match was a _____, and the
capacity crowd enjoyed every minute.

b. The Government has _____ an inquiry to
investigate leaks from the Foreign Office.

I have never understood the political _____
in America. Their elections seem to last for years.

79

c. While I was _____ the garage, I came across some gloves I lost years ago.

I had a _____ in the loft and threw out rubbish that had accumulated over the years.

d. The Council originally offered her a job, but then they _____ on her past, found that she had been to prison, and retracted the offer.

I went to the doctor for a blood test and a _____. (*Different meaning — the verb suggests that the checking is done secretly.*)

e. There was supposed to be an election, but due to an administrative _____, the ballot papers weren't ready, so the election had to be postponed.

'You mean you let the customer walk out even though you had seen him stealing something?' said the manager to her store detective. 'You _____ there, didn't you?'

f. My sister and I are very close. Whenever we _____, we have a good old chat and a laugh.

We're having a little _____ on Sunday to celebrate our good news. Would you like to come?

g. The party was going well, but suddenly a fierce fight _____ between rival gangs and a lot of damage was done.

There has been a severe _____ of food poisoning at the local hospital.

h. You paid two thousand pounds for that car! What a _____! It isn't worth half that!

Shop-keepers always try to _____ tourists by overcharging them or short-changing them.

i. No matter what I did to impress my father as I was growing up, nothing impressed him. He was always _____ me _____ by saying what he'd achieved when he was my age. I felt so deflated.

Saying that women can't handle high-powered jobs because they are too emotional is a real _____. It's simply not true.

j. Police are having a _____ on speeding motorists, and are using radar to monitor their speed.

If the Inland Revenue had more time, they would _____ on tax evaders more quickly.

k. The computer _____ the information you need when you press this key.

He had the firm's sales record over the past five years on a computer _____.

l. Customs officers are keeping a sharp _____ for the escaped prisoner in case he tries to flee the country.

While you're shopping this afternoon, _____ for a tie that will go with my new shirt.

m. Spies _____ their country's secrets.

There are many fake ten-pound notes in circulation at the moment, but the _____ is that the forgers have put Elizabeth I instead of Elizabeth II on them, so they're easy to spot.

n. Many people believe that western banks should _____ debts to third world countries, because they can't possibly afford to service them.

After the accident, my car was a complete _____ and I had to get a new one.

APPENDIX 1

Multi-word verbs

Here is a list in alphabetical order of the **multi-word verbs** dealt with in the Workbook of *Headway Advanced*.

Remember the dictionary conventions that tell you how a multi-word verb can be used.

break out	There is no object, so this is **type 1**.
break sth up	There is an object before the particle, so this is **type 2**.
look after sb/sth	There is an object after the particle, so this is **type 3**.
look down on sb/sth	There are two particles and an object, so this is **type 4**.

Items in brackets show that they are optional.

back out (of sth)	There is an object in brackets, so this can be **type 1** or **type 4**.

In this appendix, definitions are given in italics, and sometimes common subjects or objects or situations are given. The number in brackets at the end refers to the unit of the *Workbook* where the multi-word is dealt with.

back out (of sth) = *withdraw (from sth)* e.g. a promise, arrangement, deal (2)

beat sb up = *assault sb* (10)

branch out (into sth) = *expand (into a different area of business)* (8)

break out = (of a fire, fight, disease, etc.) *start suddenly* (12)

break up = (of a ship, person, relationship, etc) *come to pieces* (2)

break sth up = *smash sth* (2)

catch up (with sb) = *reach the same point, standard (as sb else)*, e.g. in a race (4)

check up on sb/sth = *investigate or examine sb/sth*, e.g. a person, a person's background or health (12)

clear sth **out** = *remove things that are no longer needed or wanted from sth*, e.g. a room, attic (12)

come by sth = *obtain sth by chance* (8)

come into sth = *inherit sth*, e.g. money, property (8)

come in for sth = *be the object of sth*, e.g. criticism, blame, abuse (6)

come in on sth = *take part in sth*, e.g. an activity, project, business scheme (8)

come up against sth = *be faced with sth; be opposed by sth*, e.g. a problem (6)

come up with sth = *produce sth*, e.g. an idea, solution (6)

count sb **out** = *(in a boxing competition) count to ten when sb is knocked down* (which means that person loses the competition) (8)

cover sth **up** = *put a piece of cloth over sth to protect it* (**literal meaning**); *hide the truth about sth*, e.g. an error, a crime, inefficiency (**metaphorical meaning**) (4)

crack down on sb/sth = *take strong action against sb/sth*, e.g. criminals, crime (12)

cut down (**on** sth) = *reduce the amount (of sth) that you do or use*, e.g. food or eating, money or spending, cigarettes or smoking (5)

do away with sth = *get rid of sth*, e.g. a restriction, rule, institution (6)

do sth **up** = *repair and decorate sth*, e.g. an old house (10)

face up to sth = *accept and deal with sth unpleasant*, e.g. the fact of no longer being young and handsome (6)

fall back on sb/sth = *rely on sb/sth; turn to sb/sth to use for support; fall backwards on sth* (4)

fall behind (**with** sth) = *fail to pay on time*, e.g. rent, payments (6)

fall for sth = *be tricked into believing sth*, e.g. a story (8)

fall out (**with** sb) = *disagree and stop being friends (with sb)* (1)

fit in (**with** sb/sth) = *adjust to match sth*, e.g. someone's plans, a colour; *feel right or good (with sb/sth)*, e.g. a person, a person's plans, a colour (6)

get away with sth = *escape due punishment for sth* (2)

get sb **down** = (of the weather, bad news) *depress sb* (1)

get off with sb = (colloquial) *begin a romantic or sexual relationship with sb* (1)

get round sb = *persuade sb to do something or agree to something* (2)

get together (**with** sb) = *meet or be together (with sb)* (12)

give sb/sth **away** = *reveal sb/sth intentionally or unintentionally* (12)

give in = *admit defeat* (10)

go along with sb/sth = *agree with sb/sth*, e.g. a person, a person's ideas or plans, a decision (6)

go through with sth = *complete sth*, e.g. a plan, arrangement (6)

have sb **on** = *play a trick on sb* or *deceive sb* (8)

hold sth **against** sb = *allow previous bad behaviour or failure to influence your opinion about sb* (1)

keep up with sb = *have the same possessions or standard of living as sb* (6)

lay sb **off** = *dismiss sb from work because trade is bad*, e.g. workers (8)

leave sb/sth **out** = *omit* or *not include sb/sth* (8)

let sb **off** = *excuse, not punish sb* or *allow sb not to be punished or to have to do something* (2)

look on sb/sth **with** sth = *regard sb/sth in a particular way*, e.g. with suspicion, disapproval (8)

look out for sb/sth = *watch* or *search carefully for sb/sth*, e.g. a friend in a crowd (12)

make up for sth = *compensate for what is lost or missing* (6)

own up (**to** sth) = *confess (sth) fully*, e.g. that you were in the wrong (2)

pack up = (informal) *stop doing sth* (8)

pass out = *faint; lose consciousness* (8)

pick sth **up** = *lift sth; acquire or learn sth*, e.g. a language, skill (4)

pick up (of the state of your health, business, etc.) = *improve* (10)

pin sb **down** = *prevent sb from moving; force sb to make a final decision or arrangement* (4)

print sth **out** = (of a computer) *provide sth in printed form*, e.g. information, figures (12)

[1]**put** sth **down** = *write sth in a diary etc. so that you remember it*, e.g. a date, address; *suppress sth*, e.g. a revolt (1, 10)

[2]**put** sth **down** = *kill sth out of humanitarian reasons*, e.g. an animal (1)

put sb **down** = *make sb seem foolish by cricitizing or ridiculing them or the things they do* (1, 12)

put sth **on** = *pretend sth in order to deceive*, e.g. an accent, tone in your voice (10)

put sb **up** = *provide a bed for sb* (1)

put up with sb/sth = *tolerate sb/sth*, e.g. a person, a person's noise, a situation (1)

rip sb/sth **off** = (slang) *steal sth* or *rob sb* (12)

rule sb/sth **out** = *consider that sb/sth is impossible*, e.g. an idea or possibility (10)

see through sb/sth = *not be deceived by sb/sth that seems pleasant or valuable etc. but it is not*, e.g. a person's scheme (4)

sell out (**of** sth) = *sell all and have none left of sth* (12)

send sb **up** = *cause sb to seem foolish*, e.g. a politician, headteacher (1)

set sth **up** = *establish* or *organize sth*, e.g. an office, committee (10, 12)

set oneself/sb **up** as sb/sth = *establish oneself/sb in a business as sb*, e.g. an architect (1)

set sb **up** = (informal) *make sb appear guilty to get them into trouble* (1)

slip up = *make a mistake* (8, 12)

sort sth **out** = *put sth in good order*, e.g. clothes, papers; *settle* or *solve sth*, e.g. a problem, dispute (4)

sound sb **out** (about sth) = *question sb to find out their opinion (about sth)* (8)

speak up for sb/sth = *talk publicly to defend sb/sth*, e.g. a person, a person's or your rights (6)

stand by sb = *help and support sb* (10)

stand up for sb/sth = *defend sb/sth*, e.g. in a fight or argument (**metaphorical meaning**) (4)

stick up for oneself/sb/sth = *support sb/sth (in an argument)*, e.g. a person, idea, one's own actions or beliefs (10)

take sth **back** = *agree to receive sth back after it has been sold*, e.g. an article of clothing that does not fit or is broken; *withdraw sth said in error*, e.g. a criticism, accusation (**metaphorical meaning**) (2)

take sb **back** (to sth) = (of music, a smell, etc) *make sb remember an earlier experience*, e.g. a holiday, your youth (2)

take sb **in** = *deceive* or *fool sb* (10)

take to sth = *adopt sth as a habit*, e.g. walking every weekend, smoking a pipe (2)

tell sb **off** (**for** sth) = *criticize sb (for sth) using angry words* or *reprimand sb for sth*, e.g. for being late, breaking sth (10)

turn out = *become different; develop* or *progress in a different way*, e.g. a holiday, the weather (8)

wear sb **out** = *exhaust sb* or *make sb very tired* (10)

wear (sth) **out** = *cause sth to become old, broken, useless* (10)

wipe sb/sth **out** = *destroy* or *eradicate sb/sth*, e.g. a village, a disease, crime (**metaphorical meaning**); *clean the inside of sth with a cloth* (**literal meaning**) (4)

work away (**at** sth) = *give continuous effort (to sth)*, e.g. maths, homework (2)

write sth **off** = *recognize that sth is a loss*, e.g. a loan; *damage sth so badly that it has no value*, e.g. a car, motorbike (12)

APPENDIX 2

Dependent Prepositions

Here is a list in alphabetical order of the **dependent prepositions** dealt with in the Workbook and Unit 4 of the Student's Book.

(to) **account for** sb/sth

(to) **agree** | **on** sth, e.g. a plan
| **to** sth, e.g. a suggestion
| **with** sb or sb's opinion etc.

(to be) **afflicted with** sth

(to be) **allergic to** sth

(to show) **appreciation of/for** sb/sth

(to) **approve of** sb/sth

(to) **argue** | **about** sth
| **for** sth, e.g. a cause
| **with** sb

(to be) **ashamed of** sb/sth

(to) **base** sth, e.g. a film, **on** sth, e.g. a book

(to) **believe in** sb/sth

(to) **benefit from** sb/sth

(to) **blame** sb/sth **for** sth

(to be) a **burden on** sb/sth

(to) **campaign for** sb/sth

(to) **call for** sb/sth

(to) **care** | **about** sb/sth
| **for** sb

(to have) the **chance of** sth

(to) **compensate for** sb/sth

(to) **compete** | **against/with** sb
| **for** sth, e.g. a prize
| **in** sth, e.g. a race

(to) **compliment** sb **on** sth

(to) **concentrate on** sth

(to) **confide in** sb

(to have) **confidence in** sb/sth

(to be) in **conflict with** sb

(to be) **in connection with** sb/sth

(to) **convince** sb **of** sth

(to) **cope with** sb/sth

(to be) **critical of** sb/sth

(to) **criticize** | everything **about** sb/sth
| sb **for** sth

a **cut in** sth, e.g. a price

(to do) **damage to** sb/sth

a **decline in** sth

(to do sth) **by degrees**

(to) **deprive** sb **of** sth

(to) **despair of** sth

a **deterioration in** sb/sth, e.g. the condition of sth or a person's health

(to) **discourage** sb **from** (doing) sth

(to have) a **discussion about/on** sb/sth

(to be) **due to** sb/sth

(to have) an **effect on** sb/sth

the **effect of** sth **on** sb/sth

(to) **emerge from** sth

(to show) **enthusiasm for** sb/sth

(to be) **enthusiastic about/over** sth

(to have) an **excuse for** sb/sth

(to) **expel** sb | **from** sth, e.g. school
| **for** sth, e.g. truancy

the **expenditure of** sth, e.g. time, money, effort **on** sth

(to) **fail in** sth

(to have) **faith in** sb/sth

(to be) **faithful to** sb/sth

(to be) **familiar with** sth

(to) **force** sb **into** sth

(to be) **fraught with** sth

(to feel) **guilty about** sb/sth

(to be) **guilty of** sth, e.g. a crime

(to **know/learn** sth) **by heart**

on the other **hand**

a **home from home**

(to) **hope for** sth

(to be) **hostile to/towards** sb/sth

(to have) an **idea about/of** sth

(to have) **ideas** (= *opinion*) **on** sth

(to be) **important to** sb/sth

(to) **improve** | **in** sth, e.g. health
| **on** sth (= *to produce sth better*, e.g. a plan)

(to) **insure against** sth

(to have) the **intention of** (doing) sth

(to) **invest in** sth

(to be) **involved in** sth

(to be) **keen for** sb to do sth, e.g. succeed

(to be) **keen on** sb/sth

a **lack of** sth

(to be) **lacking in** sth

the **likelihood of** sth

a **limit of** sth

(to) **look to** sth, e.g. the future

(to) **make** sb/sth **into** sth

at/in a **meeting**

(to recite etc.) **from memory**

in memory of sb/sth

(to be) **missing from** sth

necessary for sb/sth

(to be) **noted for** sth

(to) **object to** sth

(to be) **obsessed with** sb/sth

on my/your etc. **own**

(to be) **particular about** sth

(to be) **patient with** sb/sth

(to) **persist in** sth

in piles

(to) **plead with** sb

the **policy of** sth

(to be) **prejudiced against** sb/sth

(to) **pride** oneself **in** sth *or* **take pride in** sth

in the **prime** (of life)
(to) **protest about** sth
under protest
(to) **puzzle over** sth

a **question of** sth

at this **rate**
(to) **reason with** sb
(to) **rebel against** sb/sth
(to) **reckon on** sth
a **relationship with** sb
the **removal of** sb/sth
a **reputation for** sth
(to) **research into** sth
(to be) **responsible for** sb/sth
(to) **restrict** oneself/sb **to** sth

(to be) **safe from** sb/sth
(to) **save** sb **from** sb/sth
(to be) **satisfied with** sb/sth
(to be) **secure in** sth
(to) **seem to** sb
(to) **share with** sb
(to be) **shy** | **with** sb
        | **of** (doing sth)
on both (etc.) **sides**
in the slightest
(to) **spend** (money etc.) **on** sb/sth
(to) **stem from** sth
(to) **stop** sb **from** (doing) sth
(to be) **strict** | **about** sth
          | **with** sb
(to) **substitute for** sb
(to) **succumb to** sth
(to) **suffer from** sth

in tears
at one **time**
at that **time**
(to) **tire of** sb/sth
(to be) **tolerant of** sb/sth

in vain

(to) **warn** sb **of/about** sb/sth
on the whole
(to) **wonder** | **at** sb/sth (= *to feel*
             surprised about sb/sth
           | **about** sth (= *to feel*
             curious about sth)

over the **years**

APPENDIX 3

Linking words and phrases

The following **linking words** appear in the Students' Book and Workbook. ⟳ signifies that there is inversion of subject and verb after the linker.

Narrating

and
first (of all)
at first
at the beginning
in the beginning
then
next
before
after
after that
afterwards
when
while
soon
immediately
once
suddenly
as soon as
on
no sooner ⟳ than
hardly ⟳ when
finally
eventually
at the end
in the end
at last

Contrasting

but
however
although
despite
in spite of
nevertheless
on the contrary
on the one hand
on the other hand
whereas
while
for one thing
in contrast

Adding

also
as well as
besides
moreover
furthermore
what is more
in addition
not only ⟳ but also

Expressing cause and result

because
because of
so
so . . . that
such a . . . that
as
since
therefore
thus
as a result
this is why
consequently
for this reason
too . . . for/to
not enough . . . for/to
due to
owing to

Expressing purpose

to
so as to
in order to
so that
for (*non-specific purpose*)

Giving examples

for example
for instance
such as

Summing up/Concluding

all in all
overall
generally
in conclusion
on the whole
in the main

UNIT 1

Exercise 1

a. Ford has produced a new four-door saloon car with a top speed of over a hundred and twenty miles an hour.

b. I'm going on a three-week adventure holiday (driving) through the Sahara Desert.

c. Aiken's three-volume biography of Churchill, written in the last years of the statesman's life, has met with great critical acclaim.

d. Richard Stallman has signed a two-year record contract with EMI to produce two albums a year.

e. He wrote his employer a fifteen-page letter of resignation/explaining why he had resigned.

f. She's going to do a three-year degree course at Sussex University.

g. The first prize in the competition is a forty-eight-day world cruise on the *Queen Elizabeth II* in a first-class cabin.

h. We've just bought a six-foot pine picnic table.

i. The judge gave her a three-year prison sentence for kidnapping a millionaire's son.

j. The Midland Trading company have made a last-minute, forty-eight-million-pound take-over bid for the textile manufacturer AMA.

Exercise 2

air conditioning/air-conditioning	fire drill
airship	firework
air-raid/air raid	fire escape/fire-escape
airlift	firearms
airspace/air space	fire brigade/fire-brigade
watercolour	landmark
watermark	landscape
watermelon/water-melon	landslide
watershed	
waterslide	
waterfall	
water-wings	

Exercise 3

a. wouldn't
b. didn't may/might have
c. do
d. wouldn't
e. has been
f. had

g. had/did
h. is/does
i. wouldn't have
j. does will (or doesn't won't)
k. didn't
l. can't have/won't have

Exercise 4

a. in order to/so as to
b. as/because
c. when
d. immediately after graduating/having graduated
e. At first/In the beginning
f. Despite this/Nevertheless
g. Unfortunately
h. consequently/as a result
i. In fact [Actually is too informal]
j. subsequently
k. just before/prior to
l. On
m. However
n. to/in order to
o. Furthermore/Moreover

Exercise 5

After reading

a. A day in the life of a schoolchild.
b. Probably pre-teenage (but could be adult)
c. Verse 1 the classroom
   Verse 2 the playground
   Verse 3 the classroom
   Verse 4 Home
   Verse 5 in bed
d. giggle; squiggle; bounce; clap; slap; clatter; bang; squeaks.
e. The staccato rhythm suggests the busy nature of the day.

Groups of consonants

a. girls giggle
b. pencils write
c. bell's gone
d. balls bounce
e. hands clap
f. hand-stands
g. girls flee
h. chalk squeaks
i. Mum's got chips for tea

Word linking

a. cross it out

b. All out!

c. Best of all

d. Teacher's gone And spilt His tea.

e. Head on desk

f. Creep away

g. Dream until Another day.

Exercise 6

Matching

a. over the moon
b. on tenterhooks
c. give short shrift
d. upset the apple cart
e. learn the ropes
f. pull strings
g. be a chip off the old block
h. come up to scratch
i. go back to the drawing board
j. lick into shape

Exercise 7

a. by	i. for	q. to
b. from	j. in	r. of
c. from	k. of	s. on
d. for	l. from	t. to
e. on	m. for	u. under
f. with	n. from	v. into
g. to	o. for	
h. from	p. against	

Exercise 8

Introduction

Splash out not only means literally **to play in the water**, but also idiomatically it means **to spend extravagantly**.

Hold sth against sb has the literal meaning as in **hold the ice against the bruise**. It is used idiomatically to mean **to stay angry with someone for something they did wrong in the past**. **Fall out** has the literal meaning as **from an aeroplane**, and the idiomatic meaning of **to quarrel** and no longer be friendly with a person because of it.

Before reading

1. a. to provide accommodation for sb
   b. to go into business
   c. to make sb feel depressed
   d. to tolerate
   e. to have an animal humanely killed
   f. to write down
   g. to be put into prison
   h. to start a romantic relationship
   i. to make sb feel silly, to humiliate
   j. to make sb appear guilty of a crime when they are innocent
   k. to imitate sb in a comical or mocking manner

2.
   c. g. b. a. k. f. e. d. h. j. i.

Reading

1 He suggests the best answer to give to political pollsters is that you don't know who you are going to vote for so that they don't ask any more questions.

He suggests that Val Doonican is an easy person to make fun of. There are many popular jokes in English about the difficulties of getting on with one's mother-in-law. The teacher illustrates the meaning of **to put up with** in the context of trying to tolerate one's mother-in-law.

He suggests that the police can be corrupt, and arrange for innocent people to appear guilty if they can't find actual proof.

He suggests that American English and British English are different.

2 The teacher says I must **get off**, which means I must leave. The student has learned **to get off with** meaning to begin a romantic or sexual relationship with someone.

3 The following are taught badly.

To put down is to make fun of, but in an extremely negative way. Both meanings of **to set up** are badly taught.

To send up means to make fun of through imitation.

To get down (meaning **to depress**) and **to get off** (meaning **to leave**) aren't taught at all.

After reading

The same multi-word verb can have both literal and non-literal meanings (e.g. **to put down**). One multi-word verb can have many meanings (e.g. **to put up**). Logic often doesn't help to work out the meanings, for example, **to send someone up from prison** isn't the opposite of **to send someone down to prison**. A verb with one particle (e.g. **to get off**, **to put up**) can have a very different meaning from a verb followed by two particles (e.g. **to get off with**, **to put up with**).

UNIT 2

Exercise 2

a. were coming
b. were going to charge
c. would get
d. was leaving
e. would take
f. were going to show
g. were going to go
h. was just going to ring
i. would be
j. were going to emigrate

Exercise 3

a. 3	f. 1
b. 1	g. 1
c. 1	h. 2
d. 1	i. 1
e. 3	j. 2

Exercise 4

hop	hopped	hopping
slam	slammed	slamming
plot	plotted	plotting
stab	stabbed	stabbing
ban	banned	banning

The rule is that when a short vowel sound is followed by one consonant the consonant is doubled in the Past Tense and the Present Participle.

prefer	preferred	preferring
permit	permitted	permitting
refer	referred	referring
admit	admitted	admitting
enter	entered	entering
benefit	benefited	benefiting
develop	developed	developing

The rule is that if a two-syllable verb ends in a consonant, and if the stress is on the second syllable, the consonant is doubled. The last three are different because the stress is on the first syllable. This is true of **visit** so it's wrong to write ✗visitted✗

travel	travelled	travelling (Br E)
	traveled	traveling (Am E)
quarrel	quarrelled	quarrelling (Br E)
	quarreled	quarreling (Am E)
cancel	cancelled	cancelling (Br E)
	canceled	canceling (Am E)

Exercise 5

Practice 1

a. **At the beginning of May** is the chronological time they got married.
   In the beginning is in contrast to what happened later.
b. **At the end of the war** is the chronological time.
   In the end is a contrast to what went before.
c. **In the end** is in contrast to the awfulness of the preparation!
   At last is a long wait, and this is good news. Unfortunately, the food was cold, which is bad news.

Practice 2

a. In the beginning/at first
b. At the beginning
c. in the beginning/at first
d. finally/eventually
e. at last
f. in the end
g. At the end
h. in the end/eventually

Exercise 6

remembered	3
passionately	2
moderately	2
wizened	1
murmured	1
quivering	1
enamoured	3
deepened	1
scandalous	1
glistening	1
considerably	4
burdened	1
different	1

Exercise 7

a. obliged
b. perform
c. place
d. turmoil
e. glare
f. accompanied
g. key
h. poured
i. announced
j. afterwards
k. gather
l. anxiously
m. home
n. impact
o. appearance

Exercise 8

The following are the correct sentences.
a. c. e. h. j. k. m. n. s. t.

UNIT 3

Exercise 1

a. As
b. like
c. as
d. as
e. like
f. as/like
g. as
h. like
i. as
j. like
k. as
l. Like
m. as

Exercise 2

a. Their children don't behave as well as ours do.
b. Our garden isn't as large as theirs.
c. He earns as much in a week as I do in a month.
d. The food they served wasn't as nice as I expected it to be.
e. I didn't have as much champagne as Henry.
f. Nobody had as many mussels as I had.
g. The party didn't go on as long as I thought it would.
h. There weren't as many people at the party as he anticipated.
i. Sheila didn't behave as dreadfully as she usually does.
j. She wasn't wearing as much jewellery as she usually does.
k. I don't see as much of her as I used to.
l. The children didn't enjoy the evening as much as we did.

Exercise 3

Sample answers

a. thirty people are believed to have been injured
b. eat as much as you want
c. as long as it used to
d. he's got one in Scotland and one in Spain
e. you're sensible
f. I'm not doing anything then

Exercise 4

Sample answers

John spends three times as much on transport as he used to.
He spends fifty per cent more on entertainment than he used to.
He doesn't spend any more on accommodation.
He earns nearly twice as much as he used to.
David spends six times as much on entertainment as John does.
He spends five times more on accommodation than John does.
He earns nearly three times more than John.

Exercise 5

a. use
b. to use
c. to use
d. to use
e. use
f. going
g. go
h. go
i. going
j. to finish
k. (to) finish
l. finishing
m. to finish
n. to finish

Exercise 6

a. think   thinking
b. to forget   soaking
c. making   to make
d. seeing   to see
e. reading/to read   to rain
f. writing   to make
g. (to) find   laughing
h. to pay   to be/being
i. cooking   to cook

Exercise 7

a. turn go   f. burning
b. having   g. leaning
c. reading   h. come go take
d. coming   i. eat
e. pounding   j. making

Exercise 8

a. are getting/are going to get
b. starts
c. will have
d. is being given/will be given
e. will be/is
f. will have
g. are having/are going to have
h. are going (to go)
i. are staying/are going to stay
j. is going to start/will start
k. will have cost
l. are you going to get
m. will arrive/will be arriving/is arriving
n. does the play start
o. will get
p. will have
q. are we doing/are we going to do
h. is taking/is going to take
s. will we get/will we be getting
t. will have

Exercise 9

a. will you be moving
b. will you marry
c. are you going to accept
d. will have found
e. will be found
f. will be leaving
g. does it leave
h. will all have died
i. will have eaten   there'll be

Exercise 10

a. Because I was an only child, I was often lonely.
b. I was so lonely that my parents bought me a puppy.
c. She was in such a hurry that she forgot her season ticket.
d. I didn't have enough driving lessons to pass my test.
e. As he didn't feel very well, he didn't go back to work.
f. I'm too impatient to be a teacher.
g. Her performance with the company was disappointing. Consequently she didn't get the promotion she was seeking.
h. The car was too expensive for us to afford.
i. There were so few customers that they closed the shop early.
j. Your voice is good enough for you to train as an opera singer.
k. The book had such a profound effect on me that it changed my whole life.

Exercise 11

Stressed words

a. really did awful   g. If
b. like did eat   h. the
c. scenery acting poor   i. you
d. Peter   j. who one
e. told   k. wouldn't anyone
f. I   l. wouldn't anyone

Exercise 12

		H		D		E		U		B			
S	T	A	T	U	S	S	Y	M	B	O	L		
I		L		M		S		P		M		H	
D	I	L	E	M	M	A		T	A	B	L	E	
E		O		Y		Y		E		R		A	
S	O	W	S		P		V	E	R	S	E	D	
T		E		B	E	G	A	N		W		M	
R	U	D	D	E	R		N		D	A	T	A	
E			T		U		I		L			S	
E	R	R	O	R		S	I	N		L		T	
T		A		A		I		E		O		E	
	S	T	A	Y	I	N	G	P	O	W	E	R	
		S		S		G		T		S			

Exercise 13

a. talking nonsense
b. I'm angry with you about something, and I'm going to talk to you about it.
c. my teacher is very enthusiastic or obsessed
d. The name is familiar
e. car planned or in production
f. I'm avoiding supporting either side
g. I said something tactless
h. They speak in a confident and persuasive way
i. a narrow escape
j. to put it concisely

Exercise 14

a. on   i. of   q. for
b. against   j. in   r. with
c. from/at   k. for   s. in
d. into   l. on   t. to
e. with   m. from   u. from
f. against/with   n. of   v. to
g. in   o. on
h. in   p. in

UNIT 4

Exercise 1

a. will
b. must have been
c. can't have got
d. should/will be
e. won't have forgotten
f. will be teaching
g. should/will be
h. must
i. should
j. must have taken
k. can't be doing
l. must be
m. can't have got
n. must have been spending
o. will/must be
p. should/will
q. will have got
r. should/must have received
s. will be thinking

Exercise 2

a. may/might/could have forgotten
b. may/might think/have thought
c. may/might not have forgotten
d. may/might/could give/be giving
e. may/might/could be planning/have planned
f. may/might/could be trying
g. may/might/could have had
h. may/might/could be lying
i. may/might not have left
j. may/might/could be thinking
k. may/might not have got
l. may/might/could be
m. may/might/could be writing

Exercise 3

a. have never been able
b. Being able to
c. could
d. managed to   have been able to
e. could
f. could
g. will be able to
h. to be able to

Exercise 4

a. do we have to   don't have to/needn't   must
b. have to
c. must   had to
d. must   have to/need to
e. mustn't
f. having to
g. to have to
h. have never had to
i. will have to/must
j. would have to
k. needn't/don't have to/mustn't
l. have to
m. needn't have
n. don't/didn't have/need to
o. needn't have
p. don't have/need to

Exercise 5

a. would follow
b. *would* leave
c. would have
d. would run
e. will drink
f. *will* stub
g. *will* go
h. will borrow   will always pay

Exercise 6

a. have
b. wasn't
c. didn't
d. did
e. hasn't
f. Has
g. Does/Has
h. Was
i. Had
j. do
k. won't
l. shall

Exercise 7

Practice 1

Sample answers

a. nowadays it can be done in a matter of hours.
b. perhaps they used to be.
c. open up continental holidays to a mass market.
d. prefer to organize their own.
e. tourism reduces the differences between countries, so everywhere looks the same.
f. the other day he ordered and devoured a whole Indian curry.
g. is quite bland, the latter is rich and hot, in my opinion.
h. it only operates at certain times of year, usually during the holiday period, whilst a scheduled flight operates at a fixed time throughout the year.
i. in that Brighton is old, established and cold, whilst Marbella is new, brash and hot.
j. the more I marvel at the sights there are to see.

Practice 2

Sample answers

a. They both result in a person losing their job, but for a different reason. You are sacked if you are no good at your job or do something wrong, whilst if you are made redundant, it is not your fault at all. There simply isn't enough work for everyone and you usually get an amount of money as compensation for losing your job.
b. A dictionary and an encyclopaedia are both reference books, but the first deals solely with words and their definitions, whereas the second deals more with general knowledge.
c. They are both people that you work with, but an accomplice is a partner in crime.
d. They both entail an exchange of views and opinions, but an argument is heated, whilst a discussion is calm and reasoned.
e. They are both a means of putting words onto paper. However a word processor is much more flexible and can do many more operations with a text than a typewriter.
f. They are both a sort of journey, but an excursion is usually for one day, perhaps to the seaside and is mainly for pleasure, whereas an expedition is a sort of exploration, usually to somewhere distant and dangerous for quite a long length of time.

Exercise 8

a. F
b. F
c. R
d. F
e. R
f. R
g. F
h. R
i. R
j. F

Exercise 9

/e/	/i:/	/eə/	/ɪə/	/ɜː/	/eɪ/
bread	scream	tear	gear	yearn	break
breath	bean	pear	tear	pearl	steak
dread	lead	bear	spear		great
lead	heal	wear	fear		
dead	read		year		
spread	knead				
read	plead				
thread	bead				
instead	team				
head	breathe				
	mean				

Exercise 10

Sample answers

a. This government has shamefully neglected the Health Service.
   It has given shameless encouragement to profiteering.
   I was ashamed of my terrible behaviour the previous evening.
b. There is an intolerable level of ignorance on the subject of first aid.
   Old people can be intolerant of noisy, young children.
c. She is very appreciative of my cooking.
   There has been an appreciable increase in the cost of living.
d. He is a film critic.
   She wrote a critique on the government's foreign policy.
e. She is a very confident person, and so she does well at interviews.
   This information is strictly confidential.
f. There is a disused railway line at the bottom of our garden.
   He was jailed because he'd misused company funds.
   There is a lot of unused farm land these days.
   Or
   I found working on the farm hard, as I was unused to manual labour.
   He abused his power as head of division, and upset a lot of people.
g. My secretary is invaluable to me. I simple couldn't do without her.
   That watch is quite valuable. You should get it insured.
h. There is nothing more satisfying than looking at a well-dug vegetable patch.
   His progress was satisfactory, but doctors were still pessimistic.
i. The company has an impressive record, with an annual turn-over of over five million pounds.
   Children are very impressionable and easily influenced.
j. His letters affected me deeply, and caused me much sorrow.
   We have underestimated the effect of noise in our society.
k. The question of abortion is basically a moral issue.
   The morale of the soldiers was low, having had three months of intense fighting.
l. The principal of the college is a lady called Mary Underfield.
   Living within your means is a principle I have always lived by.
m. Coal is an efficient source of energy, but a dirty one.
   We are still looking for an effective cure for cancer.

Exercise 11

a. mile
b. rocking
c. artificial
d. sill
e. snowy
f. purring
g. home-made
h. dashing
i. grumbles
j. soothing
k. gap
l. sobering
m. fancy
n. face
o. move

Exercise 12

a. sorted it out
   sort it out
b. fell back
   fell back
c. catch up with
   catch up with
d. stand up for
   stood up for
e. picked up
   Pick it up
f. covered up
   cover up
g. pinned him down
   pinned him down
h. see through
   see through
i. wiped out
   wipe out

UNIT 5

Exercise 1

Sample answers

a. What attracts tourists to London is its sense of history, which they encounter on every street they walk down. It is the fact that it has buildings which date from Roman times that makes it such an interesting place to visit.
b. Generally, Londoners welcome the tourists, but what is annoying is the fact that normal life is almost impossible at the height of the season. It is the tourists who drop litter and clog the streets, but it is also the tourists who provide much direct and indirect employment.
c. Having tourists bring so much money to the economy is one thing, but forty million tourists a year is another.
d. What I like about London is the way you can always find some new little corner that you haven't come across before. It is the tiny back streets that attract me, not the well-publicized tourist spots.
e. Tourists find London noisy and tiring, but what they don't realize is the fact that the rest of the country is completely different. It is the bright lights of the city that they have come to see, not quiet country lanes.
f. What I can't stand is the hustle and bustle of the city, which is why I live in the country. It is peace and quiet that I want more than anything else.

Exercise 2

a. This bridge was built in 1901.
b. The escaped prisoner hasn't been seen since he knocked out a guard and ran away.
c. I've been invited to Buckingham Palace to collect an award!
d. (This is an example of spoken English, so it sounds fine. The passive would also be acceptable.)
e. (No change.)
f. Alexander Graham Bell was a scientist and inventor. He invented the telephone in 1876, and he also worked on early radio transmitters.
g. Scientists working in California have discovered a drug which stops premature ageing. The drug will be manufactured commercially, and should be available soon.
h. Reference books must not be taken out of the library.
i. The Health Service has prospered under this government. It is true that hospitals have been closed and less money spent, but the system is now streamlined.
j. (**Mrs Ethel Templeton found the tiger** and **The tiger was found by Mrs Templeton** are acceptable, according to where one wants the focus of the sentence.)
k. A few cups were broken while you were away. Sorry. We'll replace them. Apart from that, not much damage was done at all.
l. (This sentence is acceptable, given that the author has no intention of sounding modest!)

Exercise 3

a. He was sentenced to life imprisonment.
b. He sentenced her to nine months' imprisonment.
c. They show passengers how to put on a life jacket, and serve drinks and food.
d. They are shown how to put on a life jacket, and served with food, and entertained as far as possible.
e. You'll be told what to do when you arrive.
f. She'll tell you what you have to do when you arrive.

g. I was asked some impossible questions.

h. She asked me questions that I just hadn't considered.

i. He was given a lovely clock.

j. They gave him a little present.

Exercise 4

a. Shakespeare is considered to be the greatest of all playwrights.

b. He is said to have travelled widely across Europe.

c. Mrs Thatcher is said to need very little sleep.

d. He is known to have been a member of the communist party when he was young.

e. The rain is expected to disappear this afternoon.

f. The escaped prisoner is reported to be heading for Scotland.

g. She is supposed to have an income of over one hundred thousand pounds.

h. Three people are believed to have been killed in an avalanche.

i. They are presumed to have been skiing in the area when the avalanche started.

j. The super powers are thought to be heading for an agreement on nuclear weapons.

Exercise 5

a. I've been phoning Justin at the office all morning, but I can't get hold of him. And we won't see him tonight, either. By the time we get home, he'll have gone out.

b. John expected to get a decent rise because he had worked/had been working at the company for many years. He knew he sold more cars every year than any of his colleagues. He'd been selling cars all his life, and knew exactly what approach to adopt with every customer who came in.

c. A Have you seen the Renoir exhibition?
B No. Where's it on?
A At the Academy. I've been twice. It was/is wonderful. I had never seen most of the pictures. They were quite new to me.
B I'll try and get round to see it.
A By the time you get round to it, it'll have finished.

Exercise 6

a. has been proclaimed

b. was taking

c. had been pestering

d. was looking

e. turned/were turning

f. had disappeared

g. would be

h. would do

i. remains

j. prepares

k. had chosen

l. will my wife think

m. has owned

n. dates

o. had been serviced/is serviced

p. was flying/has been flying

q. was found

r. will let

s. would get

t. have never heard

u. coped

v. have made

x. feel

y. did he take/had he taken

Exercise 8

The following words are the odd man out.

a. heard   e. dull   i. minion
b. player   f. fierce   j. loud
c. sew   g. cough   k. anger
d. loose   h. lair   l. card

Exercise 9

a. It snaps/breaks.

b. crush

c. cracked

d. break

e. shatter

f. burst

g. splinter

h. crumble

i. cracked/broke/snapped

j. burst

k. broke/smashed

l. shattered

m. crush

n. snaps

o. splinter

p. crumble

Exercise 11

a. for   l. at
b. for   m. of
c. of   n. At
d. in   o. of
e. about/on   p. from
f. over   q. against
g. on   r. on
h. for   s. in
i. in   t. in
j. from   u. between
k. for   v. on

UNIT 6

Exercise 1

Sample answers

a. an up-to-date bilingual dictionary

b. a cold, miserable mid-winter day

c. a cosy, modernized thatched cottage

d. a gripping detective story

e. a posh booming voice

f. a rich filling meal

g. a loud cocktail party

h. a priceless ivory chess set

i. a constant throbbing pain

j. a wide-mouthed beaming grin

k. a quiet, leafy Victorian suburb

l. a plush, oriental carpet

Exercise 2

Sample answers

– Striking yellow plastic glasses

– Smart white cotton track suit

– Odd lace-up black leather jacket

– Unfashionable tartan and leopard skin canvas handbag

Exercise 3

a. free	f. freely	k. loud	p. wrongly
b. freely	g. wrong	l. most	q. hardly
c. directly	h. close	m. highly	r. lately
d. easier	i. wide	n. right	s. direct
e. mostly	j. closely	o. rightly	t. light

Exercise 4

1 By the way	9 obviously
2 Anyway	10 apparently
3 After all	11 surely
4 quite honestly	12 personally
5 actually	13 Generally speaking
6 Ideally	14 presumably
7 Basically	15 Admittedly
8 Naturally	16 Strictly speaking

Exercise 5

a. Naturally	f. Surely
b. After all	g. basically
c. Presumably	h. Apparently
d. Admittedly	i. Anyway
e. at least	j. obviously

Exercise 6

a. I read in the paper the other day that there have recently been several near misses in the skies over London.

b. Personally, I have never really liked travelling by air.

c. I only fly if it is absolutely essential, but even then I always try to get out of it.

d. Frankly, I just can't understand how something weighing two hundred tons can fly so easily.

e. However, I can quite understand how some people like flying very much/I can very much understand how some people quite like flying.

f. In fact, I was talking to a boy only yesterday who wants to be a pilot.

g. Actually, he also wants to go hang-gliding.

h. He has often thought about going, but he has never actually done it.

i. Even he said he sometimes felt slightly nervous at take-off and landing.

j. Fortunately, I am slowly getting used to flying, but I still don't think that I will ever actually enjoy it.

Exercise 8

Practice 1

a. The awful aunty is here in a new outfit.

b. The doctor advised me to eat only apples.

c. The author is an ugly individual who earns a lot.

d. A new Austin is too expensive for us to afford.

e. I've got three oranges for you and me.

f. He and Hugh Appleby are thirty-eight years old.

Practice 2

Quite honestly, I don't know how you've put up with it for all these years. Personally, I would have left after a few weeks. After all, it's not as though it was your fault. I mean to say, he was the one that was so keen on it in the first place. Actually, he had to work really hard to persuade you, if I remember rightly. Frankly, I think you should remind him of that a bit more often. You are still speaking to each other, presumably? I wouldn't blame you if you weren't! Seriously though, enough is enough! Admittedly, he wasn't to know, but he should have made it his job to find out! After all, he has always prided himself on his thoroughness!

Exercise 9

blood red
pitch black
nut brown
copper brown
jet black
salmon pink
shocking pink
bottle green
cherry red
emerald green
brick red
slate grey
apple green
snow white
navy blue
sky blue
olive green

Exercise 10

a. sparkling	f. showered	k. recording
b. fit	g. stipulated	l. tradition
c. address	h. viewing	m. inscribed
d. abdicated	i. bidding	n. unique
e. discerning	j. chapter	o. proceeds

Exercise 11

	¹C	A	R	N	A	²T	I	³O	N	⁴S	
⁶C	H	E		S		L		O		C	
⁸A	G	A	I	N	S	T		⁹L	I	B	R	A
R	P	T		U		L		L		R	
¹⁰N	O	T	E		¹¹S	T	A	R		¹²E	R	R
I	E		¹³S	E	E	E		Y	
¹⁴V	I	R	T	U	E		¹⁵V	A	C	¹⁶A	N	T
O			C		¹⁷E	T		D		H	
¹⁸R	O	²⁰T		C	U	R	B		²¹B	A	R	E
O		A		I		A		²²G		M		C
²³U	R	B	A	N		²⁴S	U	L	T	A	N	A
S		L		C		E		U		N		N
	²⁵B	E	T	T	E	R	M	E	N	T	

Exercise 12

Matching

cut down on

come up for, up to, down on, up with; in for, up against, away with, through with, along with.

do away with

face up to,

make up for, up to,

speak up for, along with

go up to, in for, up against, away with, through with, in with, along with,

fall down on, behind with, in with.

fit up against, in with

keep up with, in with

own up to

Gap filling

a. behind with	h. through with
b. up for	i. up against
c. up for	j. up to
d. in for/up against	k. in well with
e. down on	l. up with
f. away with	m. up to
g. up with	n. along with

UNIT 7

Exercise 1

a. Wrong — He thinks we should go and I agree.

b. Wrong — She agreed with me that we should have a party.

c. Right.

d. Wrong — She thought we should go, and I agreed.

e. Wrong — They agreed that fighting the proposal was a bad idea.

f. Wrong — Pat and Peter agree on most things.

g. Right.

h. Wrong — They advised me/us/him to try again next year./He was advised to . . .

i. Right.

j. Wrong — He advised them that they should service their car/have their car serviced every six months.

k. Wrong — My accountant advises me on all financial matters.

l. Wrong — She forced herself to eat even though she wasn't hungry.

m. Right.

n. Wrong — She forced them to give her a pay rise by threatening to resign.

o. Wrong — She persuaded me to let her go.

p. Wrong — I was persuaded not to do it/out of doing it.

q. Right.

r. Wrong — She persuaded us/everyone that her idea was best.

Exercise 2

a. I suggested that she (should) accept the offer.

b. I advised her to accept the offer.

c. I recommended that she (should) accept the offer.

d. He insisted on me settling/that I (should) settle my debts.

e. He told me to settle my debts.

f. He ordered me to settle my debts.

g. He made me settle my debts.

h. He urged me to settle my debts.

i. She said she'd pay me back tomorrow/the next day.

j. She told me that she would pay me back tomorrow/the next day.

k. She explained (to me) that she would pay me back tomorrow/the next day.

l. She promised to pay me back/that she would pay me back tomorrow/the next day.

m. She insisted that she would pay/on paying me back tomorrow/the next day.

n. She begged her father to let her/that her father let her go with him.

o. She pleaded with her father to let her go with him. (The Present Subjunctive sounds unlikely here.)

Exercise 3

a. hadn't gone

b. hadn't fallen

c. wouldn't have married

d. wouldn't have been born

e. would still be working

f. had/did

g. would be able

h. will try

i. can

j. would be

k. has worked

l. retires/is going to retire/is retiring/will be retiring

m. would have made

n. turned/had turned

o. does/is doing

p. would have been

q. could have risen

r. would have enjoyed

s. is/has been

Exercise 4

a. They wouldn't be rowing/having a row if she hadn't lost his tennis racket.

b. If she weren't a very reliable journalist, she wouldn't have been promoted to desk editor.

c. If I weren't afraid of travelling by air, I wouldn't have had to go to America by boat.

d. He wouldn't be broke if he hadn't spent all his money on a music centre.

e. If she knew anything about first aid, she could have helped him.

f. If I'd looked after my teeth, I wouldn't have false ones.

g. I'd watch the programme if I weren't seeing Ben/if I hadn't said to Ben that I'd see him in the pub.

h. If I had a video recorder, I could have recorded the programme.

i. If you weren't so gullible, you wouldn't have believed the lies he told you.

j. If I weren't going out to the theatre tonight, I would have accepted Peter's invitation to go round for a meal.

Exercise 5

a. If you happen to come across Harry . . .

b. If you should/Should you have any cause for complaint . . .

c. If the negotiations were to/Were the negotiations to break down . . .

d. If you happen to find my scarf . . .

e. If he were ever to/Were he ever to find out . . .

f. If guests should wish to/Should guests wish to have breakfast . . .

g. If we were to find/Were we to find life . . .

h. If I happen to see some shoes . . .

Exercise 6

Sample answers

a. I might go for a walk.

b. I could have given you a lift.

c. I might not be overdrawn at the end of every month.

d. they might have escaped.

e. you might get on with them better.

f. could go for a ride/drive.

g. he/she might have to take it out.

h. They could have survived if the ship had had life boats.

i. If I'd never met the poet, I might never have started to write poetry.

j. If we'd brought our swimming costumes, we could have gone swimming.

Exercise 8

/ɔː/ (6)	/ʌf/ (3)	/ɒf/ (2)	/uː/ (1)	/ə/ (2)	/əʊ/ (2)	/aʊ/ (3)
nought ought sought fought bought thought	tough enough rough	cough trough	through	thorough borough	though dough	bough plough drought
caught warn	snuff cuff	toffee off	stew queue	terror burglar	glow groan	frown doubt

Exercise 9

Sample answers

He turned on the radio to listen to the news headlines, which weren't very pleasant. 'Three people were killed in a car crash last night, and Bill Todd has been re-elected as president of the Miners' Union.' He turned the radio off. 'The news really depresses me,' he said. He gave her a passionate kiss/peck on the cheek and set off for work.

Outside it was a pleasant/hot summer's day. Brian got/climbed into his car but he couldn't start it. 'I'll have to have this car fixed', he thought. 'It really annoys/infuriates me/drives me crazy when it won't start straight away.'

He arrived at work at 9.00, and went to his office, which was attractively furnished/modern and airy. It had a panoramic/breathtaking view over the park. He took out his diary and phoned his secretary. 'Phone Mr Atkins, please.' Mr Atkins was a pleasant/valued old customer, but he always haggled about prices.

'I must make/persuade/force him to accept my terms,' Brian thought.

'Hellow, Brian' said Mr Atkins. 'I hear you've been promoted. That's excellent/wonderful news!'

'How did you hear about that?' replied Brian.

'A little birdie told me.'

'I don't understand.'

'Never mind. Now listen. Your price sounds reasonable/acceptable, but I'd like to bring the delivery date forward.'

'Now we're making progress. When to?'

'Three weeks' time would suit/be convenient for us.'

'Fine. Bye-bye. Have a good day!'

Exercise 10

a. by-product
b. by-election
c. overhaul
d. over'cast
e. overheads
f. overalls
g. overboard
h. oversight
i. over'do
j. overdose
k. understudy
l. undergrowth
m. underestimate
n. undercarriage
o. undercover
p. understaffed
q. undernourished
r. undertaker

Exercise 11

a. in the nick of time
b. sit tight
c. a month of Sundays
d. how the land lies
e. give the game away
f. smelled a rat
g. the game's up
h. spilt the beans
i. throw in the towel
j. you're barking up the wrong tree
k. you haven't got a leg to stand on
l. you'll be doing time again
m. get you off the hook

Exercise 12

a. on
b. At
c. with
d. for
e. To
f. for
g. about/at
h. of/about
i. in
j. in
k. on
l. At
m. to
n. of
o. to
p. from
q. on
r. for
s. of
t. on
u. to
v. on
w. with

UNIT 8

Exercise 1

Rob	5
Pat and Peter	9
Barbara and Tim	6
Me	7
Simon	2
Tony	4
Angela	1
Jim and Chris	3
Alice	8

Exercise 2

a. had been bitten
b. was looking
c. had been used
d. peered
e. was known
f. was going
g. was coming
h. was trying
i. had just selected
j. took
k. read
l. had just read/was just reading
m. hid/hides
n. had described
o. read
p. had written

Exercise 3

a. have ever reported
b. had just started
c. were spotted
d. were surrounded
e. to sneak
f. would be/is/might be
g. had come
h. got
i. were staying/would stay
j. to escape
k. to strike
l. believed
m. was coming

n. has suffered
o. have been destroyed
p. be predicted
q. had warned
r. were sent
s. strike
t. remains

Exercise 4

a. My children's cries of excitement woke me up with a start. 'Look, Daddy!' they shouted. 'We've found a bird's nest. It's got eggs in it, too!' 'That's lovely,' I said, 'but come away from it, or the bird will be too worried about its nest.'

b. I packed everything I needed for the journey in a small leather hold-all — books, a change of clothes, some sandwiches, and some of my mother's home-made cake.

c. The Queen who led the country during the period of its greatest industrial supremacy was Queen Victoria.

d. The Queen, who spends much of her time travelling, is well-loved by her people.

e. Mr Higgins's butcher's shop is the best in the area.

f. 'There's no point in reading that newspaper,' she said. 'It's out-of-date.'

g. The BBC starts transmitting programmes at six a.m.

h. Could you get a pound's worth of three-inch nails from the ironmonger's?

Exercise 6

/z/	/s/	/ɪz/
Jane's dog	a month's holiday	the horse's mouth
Joe's ambition	Beth's doll	Mr Walsh's car
Uncle Toby's house	the government's	the judge's decision
the boys' father	duty	Liz's mother
the world's resources	a wasp's nest	the Jones's children
	a week's pay	

Exercise 7

a – 2		i – 7	
b – 1		j – 12	
c – 3		k – 10	
d – 6		l – 11	
e – 4		m – 14	
f – 5		n – 15	
g – 9		o – 13	
h – 8			

Exercise 8

a. Twinkle, twinkle
b. dazzle
c. glow
d. flares
e. flashes
f. shines
g. diamonds sparkle; the sea sparkles
h. flickers
i. glowing
j. shines
k. flashes
l. twinkling
m. flared
n. dazzled
o. flicker
p. sparkle

	bright	dim	on and off	suddenly
sparkle	✓		✓	
shine	✓			
glow		✓		
twinkle	✓		✓	
flicker		✓	✓	
flare	✓			✓
flash	✓			✓
dazzle	✓			✓

Exercise 9

Sample answers

a. Illegal hunting for animals and fish is called poaching.
b. If you scramble over rough ground, you move over it quickly, using your hands to help you.
c. The rate of inflation; the exchange rate between dollars and sterling.
d. A seal is a large animal that eats fish and lives in cold parts of the world.
e. I put flowers on my mother's grave every week.
f. A tender smile; to tender your resignation.
g. People bore holes deep into the earth to look for coal and oil.
h. The leaves on the tree were hanging limply; a limp excuse.
i. The university was founded in 1678.
j. She tapped me lightly on the shoulder.

Exercise 10

a. humming	f. obsession	k. loss
b. Spring	g. knowledge	l. company
c. hovering	h. blood	m. pored
d. quoted	i. relics	n. set
e. express	j. inevitable	o. mere

Exercise 11

a – 3	g – 4
b – 6	h – 11
c – 8	i – 1
d – 2	j – 5
e – 10	k – 7
f – 9	

Exercise 12

a. The management laid off one hundred workers/laid them off.
b. She came into the necklace/came into it when her aunt died.
c. I've always looked on John/looked on him with great respect.
d. Before you make a decision, sound out Mary/sound her out about it.
e. How did you come by such a valuable picture/come by it so cheaply?
f. How could you fall for that lie/fall for it?
g. You must invite everybody. You can't leave out Tom/leave one out.

Type 2

The following multi-word verbs are type 2.
lay off
sound out
leave out

UNIT 9

Exercise 1

Sample answers

a. Defining, because we don't know *which* people.
b. Non-defining, because the person has been identified.
c. It could be defining or non-defining — it depends on your view of politicians. Are they *all* dishonourable, or only some?
d. It could be defining or non-defining.
e. Non-defining.
f. Probably non-defining.
g. Probably non-defining.
h. Defining.
i. Probably non-defining.
j. Non-defining.
k. Defining.
l. It could be defining or non-defining.

Exercise 2

a. The Houses of Parliament, which were built between 1840 and 1857, stand on the River Thames.
b. I gave her a piece of cake, which she ate greedily.
c. I don't like having to talk to people I've never met before.
d. I'll show you the photographs I took on my last holiday.
e. I'd like you to meet someone I've been wanting to introduce you to for ages.
f. My cat's name is Wally. The only food he eats is the most expensive brand.
g. Politicians who deceive the public are a dishonorable bunch of people. (Defining — only some politicians do.)
   Politicians, who deceive the public, are a dishonorable bunch of people. (Non-defining — they all do.)
h. My cat, who likes to sleep in front of the fire all day, is getting a little overweight.
i. The British police who carry guns are highly trained. (Defining, because only a few British police carry guns.)
j. My children, who still go to school, are coming with us on a trip to America. (This is a non-defining relative clause. In theory, a defining relative clause is possible, which would mean that only those children who still go to school — not those who have already left — are coming.)
k. He's a very happy cat. Dogs that/who chase cats are his only source of worry in the world. (Defining — only some dogs chase cats.)
   He's a very happy cat. Dogs, who chase cats, are his only source of worry in the world. (Non-defining — all dogs chase cats.)
l. Peter Smith who lives in Bradford, not the one who lives in Chester, rang you earlier. (An unlikely situation, and an unlikely sentence!)

Exercise 3

a. A man I was talking to recently told me a joke that was very funny, but which I have unfortunately forgotten.
b. Our director, whose job I applied for when the previous director left, has announced that the pay rise we asked for has had to be postponed, which really upset us.
c. The actress Joan Kelly, whose most famous film was *One for the Road*, for which she won an Oscar award, has died at the age of 77 at her home in California, where she had lived for the last twenty-five years.
d. This morning, I got a cheque in the post, which I wasn't expecting, for some work I did a long time ago, translating business texts.
e. Lord Brown, who many people look on as the best prime minister of the century, and whose memoirs, which were published last year, caused a scandal, got married today to a woman he first met fifty-five years ago, when they were both at school together.

Exercise 4

Sample answer

My wife and I have just had a holiday which your agency organized, and which I feel I must complain about. In the brochure you sent us, it said our hotel was a stone's throw from the beach, which isn't true. In fact, it is three miles from the sea, and you have to cross a motorway on which cars and lorries travel at over eighty miles an hour! What is more, the swimming pool that was shown in the picture and which looked very inviting, doesn't exist. It is a big hole in the ground, into which my children fell and cut themselves. When we came to see you, you told us about the wonderful food. You promised us it was of an internationally high standard, which it wasn't. Dinner, for which we had to wait three hours, was the same every night, and consisted of stale bread, watery soup and cold rice. I feel your company, whose motto is 'We aim to please', owes us an apology and a refund. Five hundred pounds, which was half the cost of the holiday, would be an acceptable amount.

Exercise 5

a. at the same time
b. after
c. after
d. because
e. at the same time
f. because
g. because
h. after
i. because
j. so that/with the result that
k. if
l. so that/with the result that
m. so that/with the result that
n. if

Exercise 6

a. After finishing work, he went home.
b. While eating his supper, he read a book.
c. By working hard, he saved a lot of money.
d. Since coming to live in the country a few years ago, I now realize how much I hated living in town.
e. After graduating from university, he went off to work in Australia.
f. When going abroad, it is advisable to take out travel insurance.
g. While browsing in our local bookshop, I came across a wonderful book.
h. By working hard, I managed to pass all my exams.
i. When opening a tin, be careful not to cut yourself.
j. On hearing the weather forecast, we decided not to go camping in the mountains.

Exercise 7

a. taken   taking
b. produced   producing
c. grown   growing
d. admiring   admired
e. found   finding
f. injuring   injured
g. hunted   hunting
h. driving   driven
i. seen   seeing
j. saving   saved

Exercise 9

Cried Uncle Sean, 'The earth is flat!
I really am quite sure of that.
And just to prove I tell it true,
I'll walk from here to Katmandu.
Somewhere the earth is bound to stop,
Then off the edge I'll surely drop.'
He left at five and got as far
As Dublin Bay and Mickey's Bar.
'twas five to twelve he staggered out,
Rocking and reeling all about.
At sea-wall's edge his feet they tripped
And down upon the beach he flipped.
He lay there thinking he was dead.
Then triumph flashed into his head.
'I'm right! I'm right!' yelled Uncle Sean
Removing from his beard a prawn.
Which proves that when one's had some drinks,
One can believe just what one thinks.

Exercise 10

	H	A	R	D	Y		P	R	O	S	E	
C		R		R		A		O		N		P
O	P	E	R	A		D	I	P	L	O	M	A
N		N		W		D		E		R		I
S	H	A	M	B	L	E	S		K	I	N	
P		A		D		H		E		S		
I	N	T	A	C	T		W	A	L	L	E	T
C		R		K		B		N		L		A
U	N	I	T		F	E	E	D	B	A	C	K
O		V		G		A		S		L		I
U	N	I	F	O	R	M		O	F	T	E	N
S		A		W		S		M		A		G
	S	L	I	N	G		W	E	I	R	D	

Exercise 11

a. feather
b. house
c. cat
d. Rome
e. water
f. legs
g. kitchen
h. place
i. wings
j. garden path

Exercise 12

a. to
b. with
c. from
d. to
e. for
f. into
g. from
h. with
i. of
j. on
k. with
l. for
m. about
n. to
o. of
p. in
q. with
r. for
s. about
t. to
u. on

UNIT 10

Exercise 1

a. Never again will I allow myself to be deceived in such a manner.
b. Not for one minute did she think that she would win the competition.
c. Rarely does one find a person of such integrity as Henry.
d. Not until all nuclear weapons are eliminated will world peace be secure.

e. At no time are sentries allowed to leave their posts.
f. Only after several years' training are policemen allowed to use guns.
g. In no way could I persuade her to see the foolishness of her plan.
h. His drug problem was his downfall. Not only did he lose his job, but his wife left him, too.
i. No sooner had I settled down to read the paper than the doorbell rang.
j. Little did she realize how the evening was to end.
k. Should you ever need any help, just give me a ring.
l. Had she found out that he had been married before, she would never have married him.
   If she had found out that he had been married before, never would she have married him.
m. Were life on other planets ever to be found, there would probably be no means of communication.

Exercise 2
Sample answers

Not until you get behind the wheel of the new Panama 3000 will you appreciate its elegance. When it comes to handling and performance, we've virtually cornered the market. Not only will you find that the ride is the smoothest you've ever had, but you will hardly hear the engine because of the sound-proofing we've installed. Rarely will you have experienced such luxury whilst travelling at over 100 mph. Why not take a test drive and experience the sensation yourself.

Exercise 4

a. They've put up the price of petrol again.
b. You should plant these bulbs in the autumn.
c. They've cut the flying time between London and New York by forty minutes.
d. One should always address the Queen as 'm'am' or 'your majesty'.
e. You need a visa to enter the United States.
f. One/you should wear gloves and hat to the garden party.
g. You require fresh herbs for this recipe.
h. I'd never have bought the house if I'd known they were going to build a motorway at the bottom of the garden.
i. They vaccinate most children against measles these days.
j. You can't get decent shoes these days.
k. They don't make decent shoes these days.
l. A nuclear war is a calamity which, one hopes, will never occur.

Exercise 5

It is with regret that we have to inform you that your phone has been disconnected, due to the non-payment of your phone bill. We have made every effort to establish a means whereby you settle the bill in instalments. Had you answered our enquiries, alternative arrangements might have been considered to enable you to keep your phone, since we are generally most unwilling to take this measure. However, we received no reply. Consequently, we have no alternative but to terminate your account. We intend to place the matter in the hands of our solicitors.
However, should you find yourself able to rectify the situation, we would be pleased to hear from you. We are anxious that you have your phone reinstalled as soon as possible.
A great deal of inconvenience is avoided if bills are paid promptly.

Exercise 7

a. strongly
b. greatly
c. seriously
d. strongly
e. completely
f. categorically
g. totally
h. sincerely
i. entirely
j. absolutely
k. fully
l. seriously

Exercise 8

a. terribly/awfully
b. absolutely
c. Totally/absolutely
d. quite/rather
e. terribly/really/awfully
f. very/quite
g. quite/absolutely
h. absolutely/quite/completely
i. very/quite/rather
j. quite/absolutely
k. very/terribly/really
l. quite/very/so
m. absolutely/so
n. quite/very
o. absolutely
p. absolutely/really
q. rather/quite
r. absolutely

Exercise 9

a. plain food; pale colour
b. successful attempt; modest/humble person
c. rough sea; tense/temperamental person
d. gentle breeze; lenient punishment
e. dim light; slow student
f. irrational person; exorbitant price
g. patterned wallpaper; elaborate/ornate architectural style
h. even number; regular hours of work
i. excessive amount; extreme politics
j. fake diamond; insincere emotion
k. hilly/mountainous countryside; bumpy road
l. overcast sky; guilty conscience

Exercise 10

a. handed	f. guise	k. alleged
b. treatment	g. loss	l. award
c. despair	h. rein	m. source
d. authority	i. sneaking	m. umpteenth
e. scent	j. headlined	o. invent

Exercise 11

Third from the end	ooO	Oooo	ooOo	oOo
disciplinarian	magazine	aristocrat	anniversary	museum
uncontrollable			operation	respective
imminent			competition	adventure
fertility			contemplation	inventive
comtemplate			separation	
properties			correspondent	
inseparable			celebration	
celebrate				
resident				
sentiments				
jealousy				

Exercise 12

a – 15	f – 2	k – 1
b – 4 (or 14)	g – 3	l – 13
c – 6	h – 7	m – 9
d – 8	i – 12	n – 10
e – 11	j – 5	o – 14

UNIT 11

Exercise 1

Sample answers

a. I wish he were brighter
b. I wish you wouldn't worry so much.
c. If only I hadn't overslept this morning!
d. If only she had a bit more self-confidence!
e. I'd rather you didn't drive so far in one day.
f. If only I'd worked harder!
g. It's time you settled down and got a decent job.
h. I wish he'd apologize for breaking it.
i. She wishes she hadn't drunk so much at the party.
j. If only I could give up smoking!
k. He'd rather I hadn't married Jim.
l. If only I'd been able to tell her the truth!
m. It's about time we got a word processor.
n. He wishes he could have completed it on time.
o. She wishes she hadn't had her hair cut so short.

Exercise 2

a. I don't.	g. he won't.
b. I didn't.	h. you weren't
c. I haven't/don't.	i. she didn't.
d. I was.	j. he doesn't.
e. he does.	k. she doesn't.
f. we didn't.	l. they don't.

Exercise 3

a. didn't have
b. would have liked/would like
c. could
d. hadn't invited
e. would be
f. didn't go
g. does
h. were
i. are always misbehaving/always misbehave
j. ring/rang
k. say/said
l. have/had broken
m. went
n. won't last
o. are enjoying

Exercise 4

a. could
b. was/were/is
c. did/does
d. is always going on
e. has sold
f. thought/think
g. wouldn't have done
h. I would have tried
i./j. I would love to have seen/I would have loved to have seen/I would have loved to see
k. told
l. wouldn't mind
m. listened/would just listen
n. mattered/matters
o. had/has
p. ignored/ignore
q. would work

r./s. I don't think she earns/I wouldn't think she earned/I wouldn't have thought she earned

t. got/gets

u. didn't have

v./w. I would like to have turned/I would have liked to have turned/I would have liked to turn

x. are getting

Exercise 5

a. I insist that she (should) tell me the truth.
b. He promised that he would come on time.
c. I admit that I told you lies.
d. He recommended that I (should) have the trout.
e. I propose that we (should) set another date for the meeting.
f. I am asking that you (should) allow him to go free.
g. The king ordered that his followers (should) raise an army.
h. I suggest that you (should) get an early night.
i. I complained that the food was cold and the service bad.
j. I am convinced that he is honest.
k. The company requests that visitors (should) fill in a name tag.
l. I command that every citizen (should) swear allegiance to me.

Exercise 6

a. was foiled
b. held up
c. collected
d. didn't have
e. putting/to put
f. had succeeded
g. would have been
h. was betrayed
i. acting
j. was going to take/would take
k. were positioned
l. was going to pick/was to pick
m. were allowed
n. to discuss
o. were involved/had been involved
p. began
q. were hiding/had been hiding
r. to surrender
s. were thrown
t. handcuffed (past participle)
u. were fired/had been fired
v. were being interviewed
w. will appear

Exercise 7

a. question/problem
b. view
c. problem/fact
d. trend
e. moves
f. point/fact
g. situation
h. fact
i. issue

Exercise 8

brain	reign
teeth	wreath
lost	tossed
foot	put
boast	post
suit	shoot
weight	great
slight	height
death	breath
says	Les
dull	skull
phrase	days
war	law
full	wool
chef	deaf
leaf	beef
glued	food

Exercise 10

a. life-long should mean what it says
b. priceless means **cannot** be valued
c. **Impossible!**
d. twins **naturally** the same age
e. mixed metaphors
f. unanimous means what it says
g. people don't **live** so long
h. world records have not previously been exceeded
i. twins **naturally** from the same state
j. last but by no means least

Exercise 11

a. out'number
b. outman'oeuvre
c. out'spoken
d. 'outcry
e. 'output
f. 'outfit
g. out'going
h. 'outline
i. up'date
j. 'upshot
k. 'backlog
l. 'back-breaking
m. back'fire
n. 'downfall
o. ˌdown-to-'earth

Exercise 12

a. flesh and blood
b. hard and fast
c. odds and ends
d. hands and knees
e. sick and tired
f. pros and cons
g. By and large
h. hide and seek
i. few and far
j. facts and figures
k. cut and dried
l. to and fro
m. high and low

Exercise 13

a. flash in the pan
b. tip of the iceberg
c. cup of tea
d. red herring
e. I wouldn't touch him with a barge-pole
f. head nor tail
g. spur of the moment
h. get the hang of it
i. easier said than done
j. credit where credit's due

Exercise 14

a. of	h. with	o. to
b. to	i. of	p. for
c. in	j. with	q. by
d. to	k. in	r. in
e. through	l. with	s. on/to
f. with	m. in	t. against
g. back	n. On	u. with

UNIT 12

Exercise 1

a. conditions condition	g. saving savings
b. honour honours	h. quarters quarter
c. pain pains	i. lengths length
d. terms term	j. ground grounds
e. experience experiences	k. damage damages
f. good goods	l. youths youth

Exercise 3

a. (nothing) the (nothing)	g. The the the (nothing)
b. the a the	i. (nothing)
c. The (nothing) (nothing)	j. The
d. (nothing) the a the the	k. the a
e. (nothing) (nothing) (nothing)	l. the
f. the a the (nothing)	m. a (nothing) a
h. (nothing) the (nothing)	

Exercise 4

a. However	f. wherever
b. whichever	g. wherever
c. Whenever	h. However
d. Whoever	i. whoever
e. whatever	j. whatever

Exercise 5

a. Basically/Actually	h. But/However,
b. because	i. not only
c. so as to/to	j. but also
d. Naturally	k. Anyway/Naturally
e. as a result of	l. In any case
f. after that	m. All in all
g. at that time/in the beginning	n. Personally

Exercise 6

/ʌ/ tough hiccough mother brother front monkey dull
/aʊ/ bough rounded plough
/ɒ/ cough moth bother broth font donkey bomb doll
/əʊ/ dough both dose rose comb roll though
/ə/ thorough
/ɑ:/ laugh card cart hearth clerk
/u:/ through lose wounded tomb
/ɜ:/ heard bird work word worse earth herd
/ɪə/ beard dear fear query
/e/ dead threat debt friend bury devil
/i:/ bead deed meat suite grieve fiend evil
/eɪ/ great straight
/eə/ bear pear
/ɔ:/ cork ward sword thwart corps horse lord
/aɪ/ ninth
/ɪ/ plinth sieve
/ʊ/ bull

Exercise 7

Sample answers

a. I had a stroke of luck on the horses.
b. A suit of armour.
c. To get a breath of fresh air.
d. No, just a sheet of paper.
e. No. She's never done a stroke of work in her life.
f. Yes, he gave me a very useful word of advice.
g. Yes, I am. I didn't get a wink of sleep last night.
h. No, I took it all with a pinch of salt.
i. Yes, there wasn't a hint of trouble.
j. On a plot of land overlooking the sea.
k. There was a burst of gunfire in the middle of the night.

Exercise 8

a flock of sheep
a swarm of bees
a herd of deer/cattle
a pack of cards/wolves/lies
a board of directors
a bunch of grapes/flowers/keys
a bundle of old clothes/sticks
a company of actors/soldiers
a gang of thieves/labourers
a ring of drug pushers/thieves

Exercise 9

a. bring	i. identical
b. battered	j. resurrect
c. recreate	k. tragedy
d. chance	l. test-tube
e. human	m. preserved
f. brutally	n. cells
g. specializes	o. kept
h. perfected	p. proved

Exercise 10

Exercise 11

a. sold out; sell-out	h. rip-off; rip off
b. set up; set-up	i. putting me down; put down
c. clearing out; clear-out	j. crack-down; crack down
d. checked up; check-up	k. prints out; print-out
e. slip-up; slipped up	l. look-out; look out
f. get together; get-together	m. give away; give-away
g. broke out; outbreak	n. write off; write-off

Acknowledgements

The publishers would like to thank the following for their kind permission to use articles, extracts, or adaptation from copyright material:

The Bodley Head and the estate of Charles Chaplin: extract from *My Biography* by Charles Chaplin.

Barbara Cartland: extract from *The Goddess of Love*, Pan Books.

John Cunliffe: 'Another Day' from *A very first poetry book*, Oxford University Press.

Early Times: 'Junk story that beat the experts' from the issue week ending 16 March 1988.

The *Evening Standard*: 'Give me a real old Granny' by Margaret Cregan from the issue of 11 March 1989.

Guinness Publishing Ltd: extract from *the Guinness Book of Records*, copyright © 1988 Guinness Publishing Ltd.

The *Independent*: 'The Windsor jewels, Wallis collection dazzles bidders', by Dalya Alberge from the issue of 3 April 1987.

The *Independent*: 'Three gunmen held after tip-off over £600,000 robbery attempt' by Nick Cohen from the issue of 7 April 1988.

Miles Kingston: 'Could I say to the vet, "here is my cat, please have her sent up"?' from the *Independent* of September 1987.

Gerard Nolst Trenité, whose poem 'The Chaos' (1920), provided the idea for 'Hints on pronunciation for foreigners'.

Oxford University Press: dictionary entries from *Oxford Advanced Learner's Dictionary*, 4th edition, 1989.

She Magazine: 'Flatearther' by Jack Rendle from the issue of October 1985.

Woman Magazine: 'Heard the one about Prince Charles and the aristocrat?' by Liz Porter from the issue of 31 January 1987.

World Priorities: statistics from *World Military and Social Expenditure 1987–88* by Ruth Leger Sivard, © World Priorities, Washington, DC 20007 USA.

The publishers would like to thank the following for their permission to reproduce photographs: Mary Evans Picture Library; Sotheby's.

Location photography by:
Marilyn O'Brien; Terry Williams.

Illustrations by:
Carole Gray/Allied Artists; Leo Hartas; Sharon Pallent/Maggie Mundy Illustrators' Agency; Jim Robins; Lesley Sage; Axel Scheffler; Annabel Spenceley/John Martin and Artists Ltd; Joe Wright.

Every effort has been made to trace the owners of copyright material used in this book, but we should be pleased to hear from any copyright holder whom we have been unable to contact.

Oxford University Press,
Great Clarendon Street, Oxford OX2 6DP

Oxford New York
Athens Auckland Bangkok Bogota Bombay
Buenos Aires Calcutta Cape Town Dar es Salaam Delhi
Florence Hong Kong Istanbul Karachi Kuala Lumpur
Madras Madrid Melbourne Mexico City Nairobi
Paris Singapore Taipei Tokyo Toronto

and associated companies in
Berlin Ibadan

OXFORD and OXFORD ENGLISH are
trade marks of Oxford University Press

ISBN 0 19 433564 X

© Oxford University Press 1989

First published 1989
Eleventh impression 1997

No unauthorized photocopying

Printed in Hong Kong